GROW Wellthy

THE FINANCIAL ADVISOR'S 4-STEP PLAN TO PROTECT YOUR HEALTH LIKE AN ASSET

STEVYN GUINNIP, MS, CWC

ISBN: 979-8-9929643-0-1 (Paperback)
979-8-9929643-2-5 (Hardcover)

Dedication

To my husband, Troy, whose unwavering belief carried me from that broken moment in Australia to where I stand today. Your patience and support created the space for this book to exist.

To Silas and Morgan, my greatest motivation. May this work smooth your path toward growing wellthy in all dimensions of life.

To Dad, who showed me how to serve clients with both planning and Eternal optimism. Your influence is why an exercise physiologist found her purpose in the financial world.

To Mom, whose later-in-life health transformation proves it's never too late to begin. Your curiosity and discipline continue to inspire me.

To my friend Michael Ball, whose ideal it was for this book in the first place.

To my clients. You are the inspiration and the stories in this book. You are the reason I wake up excited to do this work.

To the 508 financial advisors I interviewed for this book. Thank you for giving so freely of your time so this book could happen.

To my coach Brian Ellwood for his insights and bravery to keep asking me to go back for 'one more' book revision.

To everyone in the financial ecosystem from advisors, professionals, and business owners to their clients and families, who are working to balance wealth-building with wellbeing. May this book help you protect your most valuable asset.

Grow Wellthy Resource Hub

I've created a companion resource hub to help you implement the concepts in this book. **CoachStevyn.AI** is your personal health planning assistant who can walk you through the steps in a way that works for your unique situation. Think of it as having a health coach available 24/7 to answer your specific questions and guide your implementation. Visit the Resource Hub at www.growwellthybook.com/resources or scan the QR code below:

1-1 Wellness Consultation

If you'd like more personalized guidance, you can book a Wellness Consultation with me. We'll assess your current health, identify your highest-leverage changes, and see if working together makes sense.
Book a complimentary consultation at
www.growwellthy.com/calendar or scan the QR code below:

Foreword

My son put his newborn baby into my arms and said, "Meet your new granddaughter".

I was overwhelmed with so many emotions as I held her for the first time. I remember feeling very happy and profoundly grateful. What I remember most, though, was wondering, "How am I ever going to be able to get down on the floor and play with her? How am I ever going to keep up with the energy that she'll soon have? How am I ever going to live long enough to see her grow up?"

I was pushing 250 lbs. and had to make one of the most important decisions of my life. Am I going to be a spectator in my grandchild's life, or am I going to be a participant? I loved my life, but her arrival struck me like a thunderbolt. I need to be here to watch her grow up.

Approaching 60, I had accomplished so much, yet my weight was always a problem. Now that problem was encroaching on another important aspect of my life.

I was fortunate to be taught the information you are about to read firsthand by Stevyn. Having incorporated her wise counsel into my daily habits for the last two years, I lost 90 lbs., kept it off, and have become fit. Now, I have better focus and more energy than at any other time in my adult life.

How did this transformation occur?

First, please know that the American diet industry is not giving you the entire story. In fact, they leave important components out. What if eating less and exercising more are only a small part of the equation for you? How are you going to solve for that?

The answer is just a few pages away.

There is no big secret to improving your health. It is doing little things. A lot of little things. Repeatedly. Diets do not work, but changing your habits might.

I learned how to breathe properly, improve my sleep, reduce my stress, and live without using alcohol as a social lubricant. I learned how to incorporate many small things into my daily routine and repeat them until they became habits.

That is all it takes, but there are no shortcuts, just small changes. If there is a secret, here it is: Vitamin D- Desire, Determination, Discipline, Diet, and Dedication. These small things lead to many big things.

One of the big things for me is that every time I see my granddaughter, I am able to get down on the floor, keep up with her, and play at eye level.

Why are you a successful financial advisor? There are many factors, but a primary reason is that you care about your clients. You sincerely like going above and beyond for them. Now it is time to embrace self-care.

I truly enjoy helping others, but I used to think that helping myself in some way was being selfish in terms of the use of my time. It turns out that taking care of myself may end up being one of the most selfless things I have ever done. I can do so much more for others and myself than ever before. So can you.

We all tell our clients to invest in themselves first. Otherwise, they will never have the funds necessary to retire with enough money. Somehow, there is never enough time at the end of a day or week to take care of yourself. That is the same excuse.

After all, the biggest lies we tell are the ones we tell ourselves. Invest your time wisely and take care of yourself now. You are better than your best excuse not to.

What is your purpose? No matter what the answer is, what is your responsibility to be here to continue to pursue it for as long as possible? As you seek these answers, do not try to attempt this exploration all by yourself. Be accountable to at least one person whom you can talk to when the little voice in your head tries to convince you that you will not succeed. You will succeed, and it will be much easier if you have a partner or confidant sharing the experience with you.

Everything you need to get started is inside the pages ahead. When you read this book, you will see real people who have had their lives changed. Here are the tools for you to change yours. Enjoy the journey.

Harris Nydick, CFP®, AIFA®, is a founding partner and managing member of CFS Investment Advisory Services, LLC. With more than 40 years of experience, he provides strategic financial guidance to institutions, retirement plans, and high-net-worth individuals and families.

He is the co-author of Common Financial Sense, a former #1 Amazon bestseller that offers clear, practical strategies for maximizing 401(k) and 403(b) retirement plan outcomes. A respected voice in the financial industry, Harris is a regular contributor across television, radio, print, and digital media, where he shares insights on investing and financial planning.

Harris before we worked together.

Harris after we worked together.

Harris Nydick, CFP®, AIFA®, is a founding partner and managing member of CFS Investment Advisory Services, LLC. He generously shared his story, transformation, these images, and is the author of the foreword.

Table of Contents

Introduction: The Missing Piece

The fever came out of nowhere. Within three days, I was fighting for my life.

I had been confined to my bed, my body burning with an unexplained fever that refused to break. My husband brought me water, medication, and worried glances. The kids peeked in from time to time, their little faces showing confusion, wondering why Mommy couldn't get up to play.

We were living in Australia for a year while I launched a new kettlebell exercise program. It was an exciting opportunity that suddenly felt very far away.

I'm sure it's just a virus, I thought to myself. *It'll pass.*

But by Monday morning, the fever had not budged one bit. As an exercise physiologist, I took pride in knowing the body. But now, my own body felt like a puzzle. Reluctantly, I dragged myself to the doctor's office.

"We'll run some blood work," the doctor said after examining me. "Go home and rest. I will call you with the results."

I nodded, already picturing the antibiotics I'd pick up from the pharmacy later. Maybe I'd even feel well enough to go back to work by the end of the week.

Back home, I collapsed into bed, exhausted from the short trip. Hours crawled by. When my phone buzzed on the nightstand, I picked it up with confidence, ready for a simple answer.

Instead, I heard urgency in my doctor's voice.

"You need to get to the ER right now."

The words didn't compute at first. "The ER? Can't you just call in a prescription?"

"No. Your blood work is alarming. You need to go. Now."

My husband grabbed our kids, ages 5 and 9 at the time, and helped me into the car. The drive felt surreal. How had a fever turned into an emergency?

At the hospital, the medical team moved quickly. Blood draws. IVs. Monitors. Rapid questions.

"How long have you had the fever?" "Any pain in your abdomen?" "Are you on any medications?"

Then the doctor delivered the shocking news: "You're septic. The infection is severe. You need emergency surgery."

My husband's face paled as he juggled our confused children. I was stunned. I was supposed to be healthy, not fighting for my life.

I needed an emergency hysterectomy. The doctors had to operate before the sepsis claimed my life. I remember very little after that, except hearing the nurse say my arteries were beginning to collapse. I said a quick prayer and smiled at my young family as I was wheeled down the hall, unsure if I would see them again.

The surgery, blood transfusions, and IV antibiotics fought the sepsis ravaging my body. I survived, but those five days in the hospital aged my body a decade.

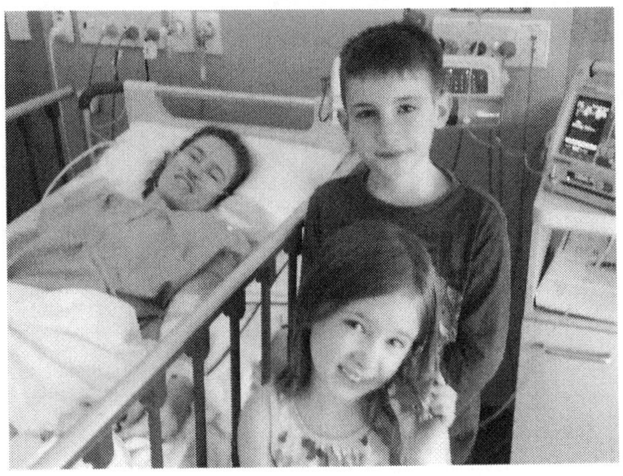

The morning after my emergency surgery in Australia.

The aggressive antibiotics ruined my gut health. The hysterectomy threw my hormones into chaos. After six weeks of recovery, I lost all the muscle I had spent years building. I developed a frozen shoulder that would plague me for the next 18 months.

In the months that followed, I began piecing together what had really happened.

My undiagnosed PCOS (polycystic ovary syndrome) had quietly set the stage for what happened. PCOS had made my hormones and immune system more fragile, increasing my risk for inflammation and insulin resistance. While the condition itself was genetic, the way it showed up in my body was shaped by lifestyle. Years of overtraining, undersleeping, and running on stress hormones took its toll. My metabolic system had been under pressure for years, and when infection struck, my body simply couldn't fight it off.

That combination of genetics and lifestyle created a perfect storm. My body was primed for burnout and finally broke.

What confused me most wasn't the sudden medical emergency—it was realizing how wrong I had been about my health. As an exercise physiologist, I built my identity on understanding the human body, yet I had completely missed how my daily habits were sabotaging my own body.

When I left Australia, I was a shell of my former self. Over the next two years, my health worsened. I gained weight, became pre-diabetic, and was diagnosed with adrenal fatigue. Each time I tried to exercise like before, I got injured. When I cut calories, I gained weight. Nothing worked.

Despite my master's degree in exercise physiology and twenty years in the fitness industry, I faced a humbling truth: everything I thought I knew about health was incomplete. I had missed something important, but what was it?

This crisis forced me to reimagine everything I thought I knew about wellness. Thankfully, I had been given a second chance. It was time to figure out what true health really meant.

Where was this missing piece? I knew exercise physiology inside and out. I understood nutrition, movement, and the human body. What could be so fundamental that I'd overlooked it entirely?

The answer came from the last place I expected: a random consulting project about massage chairs.

Finding the Missing Piece

A manufacturer of massage chairs hired me as a consultant to create educational materials on the benefits of taking breaks at work. Late one night, I was reading research papers while hiding out in my closet, so I wouldn't wake my family.

I read study after study about how stress impacts the body, and discovered something that would transform my entire approach to health: stress management and sleep weren't just "nice to haves," they were the *foundation of lasting wellness.*

The irony wasn't lost on me. Here I was, a self-proclaimed "night owl" who "worked well under pressure." I was beginning to realize that these very habits had been wearing down my system for years. It was no wonder my body eventually broke down the way it did.

This revelation was a turning point. Instead of pushing harder with intense workouts or strict diets, I began to prioritize rest and recovery. The changes started small but felt revolutionary.

I stopped viewing walking as "wasted time" and started taking evening strolls with my family after dinner. I set a wind-down alarm on my phone, though it always surprised me when it went off at 9 PM, reminding me to step away from whatever project had captured my attention. Most importantly, I started listening to my body's signals instead of overriding them.

The results were remarkable. By focusing on sleep quality and stress management, my body began to heal. I felt more in control of my actions, meals, and cravings. Even though I exercised less and ate more, I started to lose weight. Within three months, I dropped 20 pounds and reversed my pre-diabetes markers.

If a health expert could miss these warning signs so completely, I realized other high-achieving professionals might be making the same costly mistakes.

As my health improved, I felt called to help financial advisors improve theirs. This path seemed natural since I grew up as a financial advisor's daughter and had a front-row seat to the pressures of the profession.

Years earlier, I had been on a bus ride in Scotland, sitting next to one of the top financial advisors in the industry. Despite his professional success, he confided that he'd received bad news from his doctor and didn't want to be there. He was wealthy but felt poor at the same time. That image stayed with me.

I watched my dad's stress increase and health decrease during his business-building years, then witnessed him rebound after moving to a small hobby farm. The outdoor chores and fishing naturally reduced his stress and restored his strength.

I wanted to dig deeper into this subject, but found very little written information. So I started surveying financial advisors about their health. Over 18 months, I interviewed 508 advisors about their stress, nutrition, and health challenges.

The findings were alarming: their average stress level was 7 out of 10, representing chronic stress that erodes health quickly. To put this in perspective, advisor stress today is 30% higher than it was even during the 2008 financial crisis.

The irony became clear: here were experts at helping clients build financial assets to protect their future, yet many were unknowingly damaging their most valuable asset - their health.

What's fascinating is that their analytical skills make them perfectly suited to approach health systematically. All they need to do is apply the same rigor to well-being that they do to wealth management.

But what many don't realize until it's almost too late is that health isn't just another line item in retirement planning. It's the wildcard that can derail even the most carefully crafted financial plans.

Health = The Retirement "Wildcard"

An advisor recently shared a heartbreaking story with me about a couple who had done everything right financially. Jeff and Julie had saved and invested for decades, circled their retirement date on the calendar, and made detailed plans for their next chapter.

Their dreams were simple but special. After years of saving, they were ready to replace their old living room furniture and enjoy a long-awaited world cruise.

The day after Jeff retired, they couldn't wait and went furniture shopping for that new living room set. But tragedy struck. Jeff collapsed and died right there in the store.

All their careful financial planning couldn't shield them from the biggest retirement wildcard: health. They never got to enjoy the new furniture or take their dream cruise.

This story isn't unusual. I witnessed it first hand growing up in my dad's financial practice. We celebrated clients' weddings, promotions, and retirements. But we also mourned their funerals. Some were forced to retire early due to illness. Others only got "one good year" before health issues took over. Many had the money, but not the health to enjoy it.

The statistics support these observations. Age Wave, a leading think tank on aging, found what truly matters to retirees:

- Healthcare costs are the top financial worry in retirement
- Personal health problems are the leading cause of unexpected early retirement
- 96% of retirees believe good health is more important than wealth for a happy retirement

Think about that last point. After a lifetime of building wealth, most retirees realize health is the key to a fulfilling retirement. Yet our industry often focuses only on the financial aspects of retirement planning.

Health is not a wildcard. It can be managed with the right approach. Jeff and Julie's story shows us that health is a silent partner in our plans, often overlooked until it's too late.

> *"Health is a silent partner in our plan, often overlooked until it's too late."*

Your health impacts the quality of your retirement. Heather J. Barnett, MS, CFP® said it best, "*Health should be considered the currency of retirement.*"

I've seen this firsthand through the retirement journeys of my two dads. There is a big difference between living longer and living *well* longer.

The Gap That Makes All the Difference

I witnessed the crucial role of health in retirement by observing my two dads: my real dad and my bonus dad. I call them "Well Dad" and "Sick Dad."

On paper, both men retired "successfully" at the same age with sufficient financial resources. But their daily realities couldn't be more different.

Sick Dad spends most days on his couch. Medical treatments three times a week consume his time and energy. Despite having the freedom and funds to pursue interests, his health keeps him homebound. His savings now cover medications and home modifications rather than fun experiences.

Well Dad embraces an active retirement filled with grandchildren, pickleball leagues, and golf. He camps and travels in summer and enjoys Arizona sunshine in winter.

While Sick Dad navigates medical appointments, Well Dad enjoys the freedom to do what he loves.

Same age. Comparable financial resources. Entirely different retirement experiences.

The difference? Health.

This contrast forces us to confront an uncomfortable truth: No matter how much money you have, without health, your wealth loses much of its value.

In the U.S., we face a troubling reality about health. While our average lifespan is now approximately 77–78 years[23], our *healthspan*, the years lived in good health, extends to only about 64–68 years[24], [25]. This creates a gap I call *sickspan*: the years spent managing chronic diseases rather than enjoying retirement.

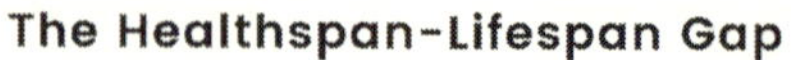

Lifespan is getting longer, but healthspan
is not, creating an increasing sickspan gap.

The Growing Gap:

- By midlife, nearly 4 out of 5 adults (78.4%) already have at least one chronic condition, and more than half (52.7%) live with multiple chronic conditions[26].

- Nationally, the average American now spends about 12 years in sickspan, the largest healthspan–lifespan gap of any high-income country[27].

During sickspan, our financial resources shift from funding enjoyable retirement activities to covering mounting medical expenses. Our focus moves from living fully to simply managing illness.

Looking at my two dads, the difference is years lived well. Well Dad maximized his healthspan, while Sick Dad's healthspan ended decades earlier.

But unlike the unpredictable market, you can influence your healthspan. Research shows that up to 80% of chronic diseases are preventable through lifestyle choices. Some people in their 80s are still hiking mountains and traveling the world, while others struggle with basic tasks in their 60s. It's about actively cultivating *healthspan.*

I began sharing this idea at industry events, and it quickly grew into a specialized practice. Financial advisors connect with my approach because I speak your language and understand the unique challenges of the industry.

One advisor who had been a cardio junkie lost 35 pounds by swapping a few runs for recovery and weight lifting. After a hip replacement, another client became a tennis coach at his old school. Through working with hundreds of financial advisors, I've discovered something profound: true health isn't found in punishing workouts or restrictive diets. It's about building the right foundation for your body to thrive.

Wellth: The Other Asset

When I talk about health as an asset, or growing "wellthy," people often smile at this play on words. But it carries a deeper meaning.

Wealth (W-E-A-L-T-H) is clear. It means having plenty of money and financial resources. Many of us aim for this, especially in the financial planning industry. We calculate, measure, and create complex strategies to increase it.

Wellth (W-E-L-L-T-H) may be a new term for you. It means having an abundance of wellness. I would argue that it is at least, if not more, valuable than wealth. It's your ability to live life fully, with the energy and freedom to pursue passions and connect with loved ones. It's the silent partner in retirement planning that needs equal attention, but unfortunately, it's often ignored until it's too late.

Wealth determines what experiences you can *afford.*

Wellth determines how long you get to have those experiences and how much you *enjoy* them.

In other words, wellth is a *serious multiplier of wealth.*

Think of these as parallel rails of a train track. One rail is wealth, the other is health. If you only lay down the wealth rail, you'll eventually find yourself stranded along the way to your destination. You need both rails to carry you where you want to go.

Lay the foundation for both wealth
and health to get you to your destination.

The retirees in the Age Wave research make one thing clear: the connection between health and wealth is crucial in retirement. We'd be wise to listen. They've already traveled the path we're on, and they're telling us that true happiness in retirement depends on both financial security and good health.

Those who lay both rails gain something priceless. They create the freedom of financial independence, as well as the physical and mental independence to fully embrace it.

The Big Swap

"Stevyn, I started in this industry with an empty bank account and good health. Now? I have plenty of money but poor health. I wish I would've met you twenty-five years ago."

These words from Andrew, one of my first financial advisor clients, perfectly capture what I call "The Big Swap." It's the process of trading health for wealth during our prime years.

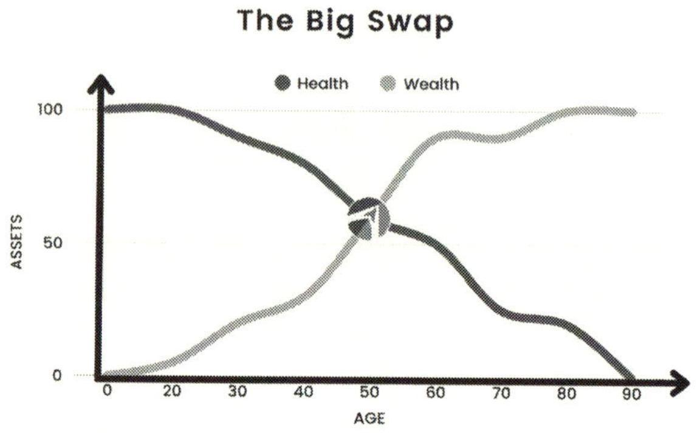

Don't make the mistake of swapping your health for your wealth.

Between ages 40-60, your wealth line typically rises while your health line drops. This isn't a coincidence.

Financial advisors often swap morning workouts for market openings and lunch breaks for client meetings. The irony is that these same advisors would never tell clients to ignore retirement savings with plans to "catch up later," yet many approach health exactly this way.

The math doesn't add up, and Andrew's story illustrates the costly consequence of this miscalculation.

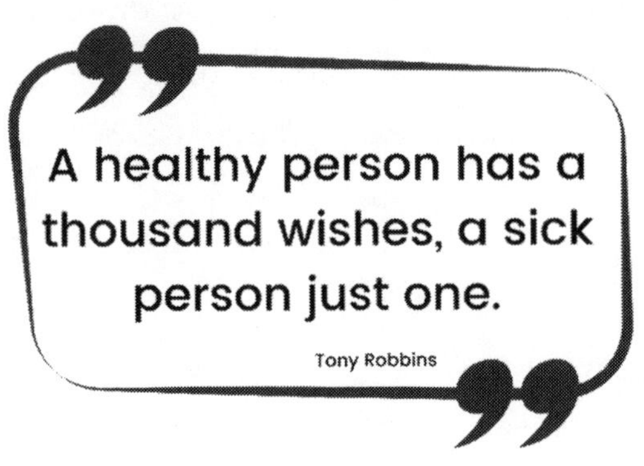

Your Path Forward

By now, I hope you're starting to see that health and wealth are intimately linked. But, you may be asking, "Where do I begin? What's the actual roadmap?"

This is where so many well-intentioned health journeys falter. Without a clear system, it's tempting to jump from one trendy diet or workout to another. It's like day trading for health instead of investing for the long haul.

Fortunately, there's a strategic approach to building health. In the next chapter, I'll introduce you to the Hierarchy of Wellth™. It's my proven 4-step framework for building sustainable health from the ground up.

I created it through my own health journey and by working with hundreds of financial advisors. It's designed specifically for busy professionals who need an efficient, high-leverage system that feels familiar to how you already think about building wealth.

You'll discover how to pay off health debt, diversify your wellness portfolio, and create compound returns that pay "health dividends" for decades. Most importantly, you'll gain the confidence that comes from having a system: a clear path forward that works with your real life, not against it.

Remember my own near-death experience in Australia? That crisis forced me to discover what true health really means. That scenario doesn't have to be your story. You can create your next chapter, one with both the financial resources to fulfill your dreams and the vibrant health to enjoy them.

The journey to wellth starts now.

CHAPTER 1

Introducing The Hierarchy of Wellth

Sarah, a driven advisor with two young kids, seemed to be doing all the right things. She woke up at 5 AM for workouts, followed strict meal plans, and tracked every calorie. Yet, her blood work continued to get worse, and the numbers on the scale kept climbing.

Then, her energy crashed.

"I know I should get up early to exercise," she said during our first meeting. Exhaustion was clear in her voice. "But I can't seem to drag myself out of bed anymore."

Sarah's story reflects a pattern I see constantly with financial advisors. They approach health the way many people approach investing, jumping straight into aggressive actions without doing the first things first. They try to outrun poor habits with intensity, much like trying to invest their way out of credit card debt.

The result? Diminishing returns, frustration, and eventually giving up entirely.

But what if Sarah's problem wasn't her effort or dedication? What if she was simply doing things in the wrong order?

Why Order Matters

Have you ever noticed how your most successful clients didn't build wealth randomly? They followed a clear order, establishing emergency funds before aggressive investments, paying off high-interest debt before adding to retirement accounts, and securing insurance before purchasing luxuries.

I've got good news—health follows the *same* core philosophy.

Think of your health like building a house. Would you hang drywall before framing the walls? Install appliances before running electricity? Of course not. Each phase builds upon the previous one, creating a structure that can withstand life's challenges.

Most health approaches fail because they violate this fundamental principle of *sequence*. They promote tough workouts before building recovery skills. They suggest strict diets before tackling the stress that causes cravings.

For Sarah, everything changed when she learned that forcing her morning workouts when she was tired was disrupting the order of healthy habits. She shifted from punishing herself to being strategic and moved from fighting her body to partnering with it.

Sarah's breakthrough came from following a specific sequence: a framework I developed after working with hundreds of financial advisors through their health transformations—The Hierarchy of Wellth™

The Hierarchy of Wellth™

The Hierarchy of Wellth™ is a powerful 4-step framework that builds lasting health using the same core principles that create lifelong wealth.

This pyramid is like Maslow's hierarchy of needs. It builds upon itself, one layer at a time. You start at the bottom and move upward. However, unlike Maslow's model, you don't stop at the top. You keep cycling through all four levels, strengthening your foundation as you build upward.

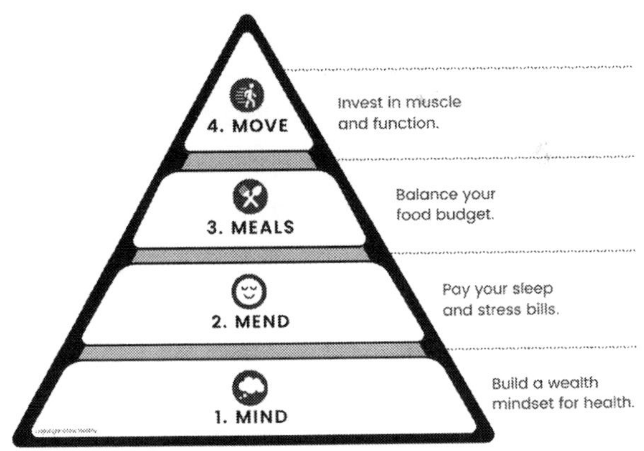

The four levels of health work best together and in the right order.

The Four Levels

Level 1: Mind - Build a Wealth Mindset for Health

Your mindset is your investment strategy for health. It shapes how you read your body's signals and make decisions. You wouldn't create a financial plan without knowing a client's goals and risk tolerance, yet we often approach health without this essential groundwork. A solid investment philosophy guides every financial choice. Similarly, a healthy mindset influences all your health decisions. Without it, even the best strategies will fail over time.

Level 2: Mend - Pay Your Sleep and Stress "Bills"

Once your mindset is aligned, focus on recovery by systematically paying off "health debt" you've accumulated through poor sleep and chronic stress. Just like aggressively investing while carrying crushing credit card debt doesn't make sense, trying to build health while carrying massive sleep and stress debt is mathematically impossible. Your body's "interest payments" on these debts consume resources that could otherwise go toward building health.

Level 3: Meals - Balance Your Food Budget

With your mindset set and recovery on track, you can focus on nutrition. Like a well-diversified investment portfolio, your nutritional approach should balance different "asset classes," allocate resources based on your body's unique needs, and adjust strategies as conditions change. Food is information that tells your body whether to store or burn, inflame or heal, build or break down.

Level 4: Move - Invest in Muscle and Function

This is your growth strategy. Movement builds capacity for the life you want to live. Think of it as your growth investments: daily activity (small deposits that add up), strength training (builds long-term resilience), and mobility work (prevents catastrophic losses from injury).

How to Track Your Progress

The Hierarchy of Wellth™ is based on a simple 1-10 scoring system where you can take an assessment, get your score on each of the four areas, and understand where you are and where you're headed.

Health Continuum

Rate Your Health on this Scale of 1-10.

Struggling | Inconsistent | Strong

0 1 2 3 4 5 6 7 8 9 10

Your health score is important, but knowing what direction it's heading matters more.

1-3: Struggling. This area needs immediate attention

4-6: Inconsistent. You have some good habits, but lack a systematic approach

7-9: Strong. You're doing well and seeing results
10: Optimized. This area is working effortlessly for you

You're only as strong as your weakest score. If your Mind is an 8, Mend is a 3, Meals is a 7, and Move is a 6, then sleep and stress management are limiting everything else. That's where you need to focus first.

Throughout this book, you'll assess each area individually and learn how they work together. Each section includes tools to measure your current position and strategies to improve your score in that specific area.

The direction you're heading matters more than your starting number. Maybe you're at a 3 or 4 and dealing with health challenges. You can still take steps toward improvement. Small, consistent health habits create remarkable returns over time.

Time of Day Matters

Here's something crucial that makes this framework even more powerful: *when* you implement these practices matters as much as *what* you do. Your body responds differently throughout the day, so doing healthy habits at the right time of the day can make them feel effortless rather than forced.

As we explore each level, you'll discover how to align your efforts with your natural rhythms.

So, expect some guidance on not only *what* to do, but *what time of day* to do it.

Your Path Forward

You can use the same framework Sarah discovered: the Hierarchy of Wellth™. You can achieve health through careful planning, not random actions, using the same systematic approach you use to build wealth.

In the following chapters, I'll take you through each level of the hierarchy, giving you the key concepts and actionable steps for each of the four levels. You'll learn how to assess where you are, make smart decisions, and build sustainable habits that compound over time.

PART 1

MIND

Harris leaned back in his chair, smiling as he pulled up photos from his recent hiking trip in Africa. A year ago, he couldn't get down on the floor to play with his granddaughter. Now he was hiking mountains on the other side of the world.

Harris ranked among the top advisors on Forbes' and Barron's lists and was used to tracking metrics and measuring success. Yet, the numbers he cherished now had nothing to do with AUM (assets under management).

When we first assessed Harris on the Hierarchy of Wellth, he was a 5 overall. A year later, he had reached an 8.

Harris before we worked together. **Harris after we worked together.**

Harris before and after working together.

Harris Nydick, CFP®, AIFA®, is a founding partner and managing member of CFS Investment Advisory Services, LLC. He generously shared his story, transformation, these images, and is the author of the foreword.

His transformation was remarkable:

- 90 pounds lost
- Blood pressure normalized (no medication needed)
- All five markers of metabolic health back in optimal ranges

But the most powerful change wasn't measured in pounds or lab results. It was measured in energy, confidence, and presence. With renewed vitality, Harris reclaimed his role as an active participant in his family's life.

That trip to Africa? A year earlier, it would have felt impossible.

And here's the key: Harris's transformation didn't start with food or exercise. It started in his *mind.*

Mindset's Place in Your Hierarchy of Wellth

This is precisely why the Mind level forms the base of the Hierarchy of Wellth. Like any solid structure, lasting health begins with proper groundwork.

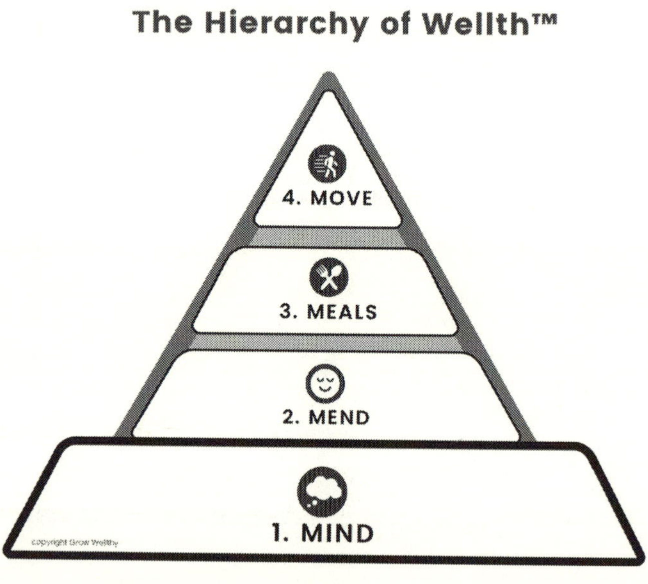

The Hierarchy of Wellth™

4. MOVE

3. MEALS

2. MEND

1. MIND

copyright Grow Wellthy

"Mind" is the base of the Hierarchy of Wellth and the first area to focus on.

Think of your mind as the operating system that runs every health decision you make. You can't build sustainable health without first addressing how you think about your body and your wellbeing. And how you think is how your health will go.

I know part of you might be thinking, *"Can we skip to the food and exercise part?"*

But here's what I've learned after coaching hundreds of financial professionals: those who try to bypass this step inevitably hit a wall.

Harris didn't succeed because he found the perfect diet or workout routine. He succeeded because he developed the right mental framework for making health decisions. Without that groundwork, even the best tactics eventually crumble under life's pressures.

Harris' Why: The Fuel for Change

For Harris, it started with getting clear on his *why*. He was sick and tired of feeling sick and tired. And he wanted to be the kind of grandfather who was a participant, not a spectator.

That clarity became the fuel that powered his daily choices. When willpower would have failed, his deeper purpose carried him forward.

What's your health *why*? Maybe it's being present and energetic for your family, having stamina to serve clients at your highest level, avoiding the struggles you watched your parents face, or simply feeling confident and strong in your body. Your why doesn't need to be profound or unique. It just needs to be true for you.

From Why to Goals

A strong why is powerful, but it needs direction. Harris translated his why into clear, specific goals: getting on the floor with his granddaughter and getting off blood pressure medication. Those weren't vague wishes; they were targets that guided his daily choices.

Harris figured this out intuitively, but you can be more systematic about it by asking three simple questions:

- Where is my health holding me back right now?
- What would thriving look like for me, both today and in the future?
- How can I connect those goals to what matters most in my life?

When you combine your why with clear goals, your health decisions stop being about willpower and start being about purpose.

Laying the Groundwork

Harris's journey shows us what's possible when you start with mindset. He uncovered his why and then set clear goals. Finally, he built a framework for making decisions he could trust. In the next three chapters, you'll learn how to do the same.

- Chapter 4: how to stop fighting your body and start partnering with it

- Chapter 5: how to treat your health like an asset, just as you do with finances
- Chapter 6: how to know your numbers so you can make informed, confident choices

Together, these tools will give you both the motivation and the decision-making confidence to create lasting change.

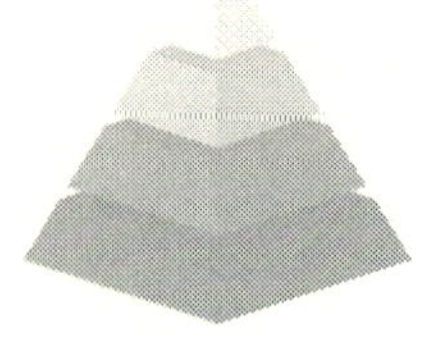

CHAPTER 2

Become a Partner

"That's a boy's name!"

These words echoed throughout my childhood as I navigated life with an unusual name - Stevyn. Growing up in the 1970s and 80s, I desperately wanted to fit in. But two things constantly made me stand out: my name and my height.

While my friends had names like Jennifer, Amy, and Michelle, I was stuck with a name that always needed explaining. Teachers stumbled over it during roll call. Kids would snicker, and I constantly found myself correcting people on how it was spelled (but that only drew more attention).

Making matters worse, I was taller than almost everyone in my class, including boys and even some teachers. By junior high, I had already reached 5'7", and I eventually topped out at 5'10". In an era when girls were expected to be petite, I towered over my peers. I couldn't hide in class photos. I couldn't blend into a crowd. I felt like a walking exclamation point in a world of periods.

All I wanted was to be normal, average, and unremarkable. Anything but the tall girl with the weird name.

For years, I fought against these qualities and spent enormous energy battling who I naturally was, convinced that my differences were problems to solve.

Now at 50, running a health coaching business for financial advisors and their clients, I still get comments about my name and height. But something remarkable happened when I stopped fighting these traits and started working with them.

My unusual name helps people remember me in a crowded marketplace. My height gives me presence when speaking to groups. The very attributes I once saw as liabilities have become professional assets.

The transformation didn't happen because I changed who I was. It happened because I changed how I related to who I was. I shifted from opponent to partner.

Why Partnership Thinking Transforms Health

This same shift transforms your relationship with health. Many of us approach our bodies like I approached my name, as something to fight against, criticize, and try to force into submission. We battle symptoms instead of listening to them. We ignore signals instead of partnering with them.

When you stop fighting your body and start listening to it as an ally, health becomes less of a struggle and more of a natural conversation. You begin working with your body's signals instead of against them.

Your body is incredibly intelligent. It's constantly adapting, healing, and working to keep you alive. When you view it as a partner rather than an opponent, you tap into wisdom that no external program can provide.

Applying Partnership Across the 4M's

This partnership mindset isn't just a feel-good idea. It's practical. It changes the way you approach every other area of health.

- **Mend (sleep & stress):** Instead of forcing rigid bedtime rules, you tune into your body's natural rhythms and create conditions that support recovery.
- **Meals (nutrition):** Instead of following restrictive diets, you notice how foods affect your energy and mood and make choices that sustain you.
- **Move (exercise & mobility):** Instead of punishing yourself with workouts you hate, you choose activities that feel sustainable and enjoyable.

When you take this partner approach, healthy habits stop feeling like battles of willpower. They become natural extensions of who you are.

Two Essential Components

To live in true partnership with your body, you need two things working together:

- **Awareness.** An honest assessment of where you are, through data and self-observation.
- **Curiosity.** Openness to experiment, explore, and adjust without judgment.

Awareness without curiosity becomes another weapon for self-criticism. Curiosity without awareness leads to wandering without direction. Together, they create lasting transformation so you can improve your health scores across all areas.

Tools for Practicing Partnership

Here are a few practical ways to strengthen this mindset:

- **Become a Feel-Good Detective.** Instead of forcing yourself into habits you hate, experiment with what makes you feel both good and good *for you.* Swap "shoulds" for discoveries.
- **Reframe Limiting Beliefs.** Notice your inner dialogue and swap self-criticism for empowering alternatives. "I'm lazy" becomes "It's not a priority for me right now." "My body is broken" becomes "I'm in the process of healing."

Instead of...	Reframe as...
I don't have time for health.	I can't afford to skip it because it supports everything else I want.
I've tried everything, and nothing works	I haven't found my unique path yet, but every attempt teaches me something valuable.
I have to finish all the food on my plate.	I love my mom, but she was wrong, and I need to listen to my hunger and fullness cues.
I don't have time for a full workout, so I'll skip it.	Every healthy action counts, so I will do what I can in the 10 minutes I have.

- **Ask Curious Questions.** When you get stuck, ask: *"I wonder why this approach isn't working for me?"* or *"What would it be like to try___?"*Curiosity lowers resistance and opens space for new possibilities.

Partnership is Your Bridge to Success

This partnership mindset is the bridge between knowing what to do and actually doing it. It ensures that the strategies you'll learn in the upcoming chapters don't become rigid checklists, but instead flow naturally into your life. Health stops being a struggle. It becomes a collaboration. One that can sustain you for decades to come.

CHAPTER 3

Treat Your Health Like an Asset

Mike, a financial advisor I interviewed during my research for this book, prided himself on tracking every financial metric for his clients. He monitored portfolios, calculated net worth, and projected retirement needs with precision.

Yet when it came to his own health, Mike ignored the warning signals: chest pain during stress, gradual weight gain, predictable afternoon fatigue. He pushed them aside in favor of "more important" priorities.

One afternoon, while advising a young client on the cost of delaying retirement savings, Mike had a moment of stark clarity. He was making the same expensive mistake with his health that he warned clients against with their finances.

That evening, he did something only a financial advisor would think to do. He grabbed a sheet of paper, wrote "Health Balance Sheet" across the top, and drew a line down the middle: Assets on the left, Liabilities on the right.

In minutes, he could see the truth. His assets, good sleep, gym visits, no medications, were outweighed by liabilities like stress, skipped meals, and 20 extra pounds.

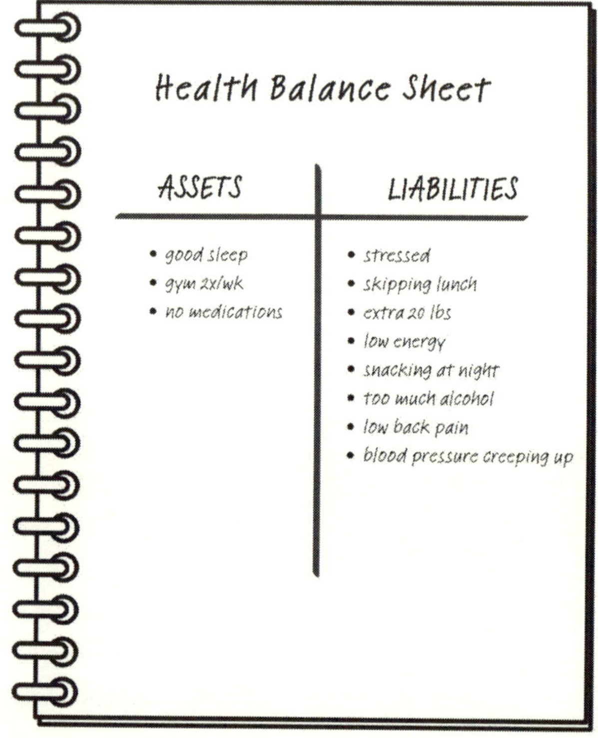

A Health Balance Sheet is a simple way to quickly assess your current status.

It was a situation he would never tolerate in a portfolio, yet here it was staring back at him in his own health. The next morning, Mike scheduled a recurring 30-minute walk on his calendar.

Your Health Balance Sheet

Mike's simple exercise works because it borrows a familiar financial principle: assets minus liabilities = net worth. In health, every choice you make either builds your assets or adds to your liabilities.

- **Health Assets** build value over time.
- **Health Liabilities** drain your reserves.

This simple way of thinking about your health helps you see why your health may feel misaligned. Often, liabilities are quietly outweighing assets.

Take a few minutes to draw your own health balance sheet. Then write down everything you can think of that is going well under the "assets" column. These could be things like "not on any medications, like to walk after dinner, sleep great."

Then list all the things that are negatively impacting your health. Things like "high stress, frequent stomach aches, and drinking more alcohol than I should."

Be honest and thorough. You may be surprised by what you discover.

Other Financial Principles That Apply to Health

The balance sheet is just the start. Other concepts you already know as an advisor also apply to health:

- **Pay Yourself First:** Schedule health like you schedule client meetings. You don't "find time" for retirement savings. You make it automatic. Do the same with sleep, meals, and movement.

- **Compound Returns:** Small daily investments outperform sporadic, intense efforts. A 10-minute walk every day beats a once-a-month marathon gym session.

- **Diversification:** No single habit protects against all risks. Balancing your portfolio across the 4M's (Mind, Mend, Meals, Move) is how you move into the "strong" zone on the health continuum.

- **Risk Management:** Healthy habits are insurance policies against chronic disease. The premium you pay today prevents catastrophic costs later.

A Due Diligence Framework for Health Decisions

Financial advisors don't make portfolio moves without due diligence. The same applies to your health. Before adding a new habit, diet, or exercise, run it through these three checks:

1. **Does this solve a real problem?**
   Your body is constantly sending messages. Instead of dismissing symptoms as "just getting older," ask: *What is my body trying to tell me?*

2. **Is there evidence that it will work?**
   Research is like your market map—it shows the terrain. Ask: *What does the science say, and does it apply to me right now?*

3. **Does it fit my life?**
   A strategy that doesn't align with your lifestyle won't last. Ask: *Does this fit how I actually live?*

When all three checks align, you've found the sweet spot where your body's needs, solid evidence, and real life intersect. That's when change sticks.

A Daily Compass for Small Choices

Of course, not every decision requires a full analysis. Sometimes it's as simple as standing in the kitchen at 9 PM, wondering what to do next.

For those moments, I lean on the wisdom of my mentor, Dr. Brad Cooper, CEO of Catalyst Coaching 360 who was previously highlighted as the "World's Fittest CEO."

He told me:

"We aren't seeking perfection. Rather, we're aiming to be intentional in our lives by asking two questions:

1. Will this choice make me better or worse tomorrow?

2. Is it worth it?"

These two questions turn rigid rules into thoughtful trade-offs. They let you enjoy life while still protecting your health. Examples might include deciding when to enjoy a glass of wine, or when to trade out an interval session for a walk with the dog (without guilt).

Think of the three checks as your *due diligence* for major health decisions, and Dr. Cooper's two questions as your *daily compass* for the small ones. Together, they give you both strategic direction and practical flexibility.

The Cost of Ignoring Your Health Investment

Remember: the #1 cause of unplanned early retirement isn't market downturns or job loss—it's health problems. Ignoring your health creates a triple hit:

- Lost income during peak earning years
- Early withdrawals with penalties, taxes, and lost compounding
- Rising healthcare expenses that erode financial security

That's why the most powerful asset you can invest in is your health.

Kevin's Story: Proof in Practice

Kevin, a financial advisor of 37 years, discovered this firsthand. After a hip replacement and months of caring for sick family members, he was worn down. After his physical, Kevin said, "Everything was borderline this and borderline that."

When he attended one of my webinars, the concept of "health debt" clicked. Kevin realized he needed to apply the same investment principles he taught clients to his own well-being.

He began viewing each daily choice as either an *investment* in or a *withdrawal* from his health. The results were remarkable.

Six months later, Kevin had:

- Lost over 40 pounds
- Dropped six inches from his waist
- Turned his borderline lab results into normal ranges

But the biggest dividend wasn't measured in pounds or inches. With his new energy and mobility, Kevin returned to the tennis court and even became the coach at his old high school.

"When they asked me to coach, I almost laughed," he told me. "Six months earlier, I just wanted to get back on the courts. Now I'm running drills with teenagers."

That's the power of treating your health like an asset. Just like Kevin, you can begin compounding returns today by investing consistently, managing risk wisely, and using the right decision-making tools.

CHAPTER 4

Know Your Numbers

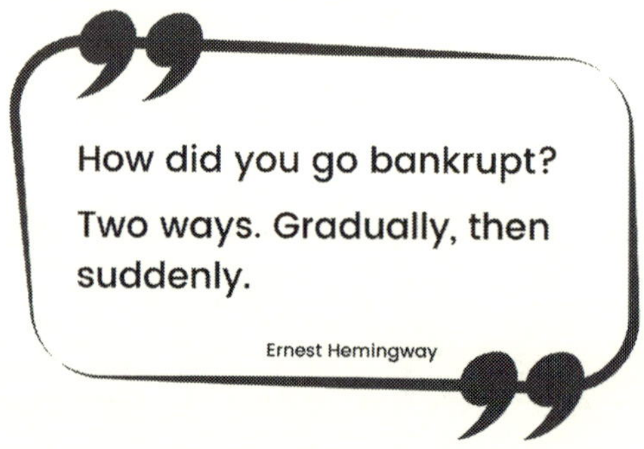

David often told his clients, "You can't manage what you don't measure," especially if they were resisting tracking their expenses or reviewing their statements.

Yet, when I asked him to rate his health on the continuum, he said, "I'm not really sure. It's not perfect, but not too bad. I'd give myself a 7 out of 10 because I'm not on any medications like most of my friends are."

That's the equivalent of one of his clients saying, "My finances aren't too bad because I drive a nicer car than most of my friends."

When I asked him when his last blood work was done, he couldn't remember. "Probably three years ago?" he guessed. "Everything was fine then."

He agreed it was time to get some new labs drawn. That's when he found out his triglycerides were high, his blood pressure was elevated, and his fasting glucose put him in the pre-diabetes range.

Three of his five metabolic health markers (more on that soon) had shifted into the danger zone without him knowing. He was now in health debt.

"If this were a client's portfolio," David realized, "I'd be calling an emergency meeting."

The irony wasn't lost on him. He'd never let a client fly blind with their finances, yet that's exactly what he'd been doing with his health.

When David started paying attention to and tracking his health metrics, he thought he would feel stressed or guilty, but instead, he felt relief. He finally had data he could work with.

"It's the same feeling I get when I help a client organize their financial picture," David explained. "Once you know where you stand, you can make a plan."

Within six months of starting a few targeted changes based on his metrics, David's blood pressure normalized, his triglycerides dropped to better-than-normal levels, and his glucose returned to healthy ranges. But the biggest change was *psychological.*

"I'm not wondering anymore," he said. "I'm not lying awake at night worried about what might be happening inside my body. I know my numbers, I track the trends, and I can make adjustments before small problems become big ones."

This is the power of health metrics done right. They don't create anxiety; they eliminate it. They give you the same confidence in your health decisions that you have in your financial decisions.

Remember how David originally rated his health as a 7 on the continuum? That was before he went through each of the 4M levels or understood his numbers. He admitted he was probably more like a 5 or 6 when he started. Comparing himself to his friends wasn't a reliable assessment method.

Your High 5 Metabolic Health Audit

After you have an idea of where you are on the continuum, it's time to establish your baseline metrics with the "High 5." These are five essential markers that provide a snapshot of your metabolic health (how well your body uses and stores energy).

Tracking these five markers gives you an early warning system for what Dr. Peter Attia, author of Outlive, calls the four horsemen of chronic disease: heart disease, type II diabetes, cancer, and dementia.

Dr. Casey Means, author of Good Energy, notes that 92% of middle-aged Americans don't meet these five criteria:

- **HDL cholesterol:** >40 mg/dL (men), >50 mg/dL (women)
- **Triglycerides:** <150 mg/dL
- **Fasting blood glucose:** <100 mg/dL
- **Blood pressure:** <130/85 mmHg
- **Waist circumference:** <40 inches (men), <35 inches (women)

The goal is to see how many you have, and then to earn back or protect all five for as long as possible. Even if you meet all five and are part of the 8% of metabolically healthy people, it can change quickly. That's why I encourage you to track your trends on each of these. But don't worry about collecting your numbers yet. I'll walk you through this process in the next chapter.

The High 5 gives you a quick snapshot of your metabolic health, but there's much more to explore when you're ready. For my clients who want a deeper understanding, I recommend a comprehensive metabolic panel that includes markers like fasting insulin, vitamin D, inflammatory markers, and advanced lipid profiles.

Body composition analysis can also provide valuable insights beyond what the scale shows by tracking muscle mass, body fat percentage, and metabolic age.

This book focuses on the essential metrics that matter most, but if you want detailed guidance on comprehensive testing and interpreting advanced markers, I've got you covered. I created the Grow Wellthy Resource Hub that includes my favorite lab tests and assessment tools to help you take your numbers to the next level.

Remember David's wake-up call? His triglycerides were high, his blood pressure was up, and his glucose was headed toward diabetes. Three out of these five markers had moved into the danger zone. If David had been tracking these annually, he could have made adjustments sooner.

How to Approach Your Numbers

Metrics are tools, not judges. Approach your numbers with curiosity, not judgment. This prevents the common trap of obsessing over data while ignoring your body's actual experience.

Essential principles for metric success:

- **Focus on trends, not daily fluctuations.** Your body naturally varies day to day.
- **Celebrate improvements, not just ideal numbers.** Progress matters more than perfection.
- **Use metrics as feedback, not validation.** Numbers don't define your worth, only your current position.
- **Start small.** Begin with just a few key metrics rather than tracking everything at once.

The goal is to develop enough awareness of your numbers that you can make informed decisions about your health early and often.

CHAPTER 5

Mind Toolkit

Rachel, a financial planner from Denver, laughed when I asked if she had a plan to reach her health goals.

"I'm staring at two documents on my desk," she said. "One is a detailed financial plan I created for a client yesterday. It has everything, goals, risk assessment, and a detailed roadmap for this couple to retire in five years."

She continued, "And the other one is a crumpled sticky note with 'lose 15 pounds' scribbled on it. That's my entire approach to health planning."

The contrast was stark. Rachel could create sophisticated wealth-building strategies for her clients, but when it came to her own health, she was operating *without any system at all.*

You now have something Rachel didn't: a complete Mind toolkit.

You know that how you *think* about your health will make everything else work. Let's put these pieces together so you can move forward with confidence.

Your Mind Assessment

Rate your MIND health by scoring yourself on four questions:

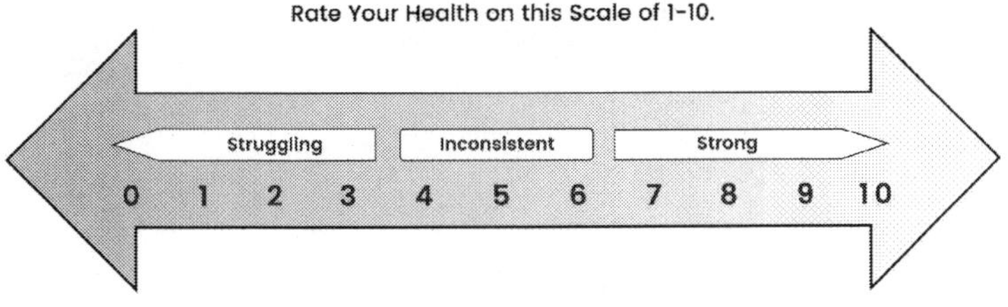

1. ______ **How structured is your wellness plan?**

1-3 = No health plan, no defined goals, winging it

4-6 = Vague health intentions, no structured approach

7-9 = Clear wellness plan, defined goals, mostly following it

10 = Detailed wellness plan, perfectly executed

2. ______ **How well do you understand and manage your health?**

1-3 = Unknown or unmanaged conditions/risks

4-6 = Diagnosed, mostly managed conditions/risks

7-9 = Clear understanding of key metrics, trends, comfortable with health

10 = Optimal health markers, 100% preventive mindset

3. ______ **How well do you make health choices?**

1-3 = Reactive, emotion-driven health decisions

4-6 = Sometimes strategic, often impulsive

7-9 = Usually strategic, clear decision framework

10 = Always strategic, automatic healthy choices

4. _____ How well do you partner with your body on health challenges?

1-3 = Fight against body, see health as punishment/project to fix

4-6 = Sometimes curious, but often frustrated or critical

7-9 = Generally curious and supportive, find ways that feel good

10 =Complete partnership, approach health with curiosity and joy

_____ Total / 4 = _______ MIND Score

Your Mind Action Plan

Complete these mindset exercises:

Clarify your why. What is your deeper motivation for getting healthy?

____

____

____

Set 1-3 meaningful health goals:

1. ______________________________
2. ______________________________
3. ______________________________

Create your Health Balance Sheet (quick list of assets vs. liabilities).

Determine your High 5 Metabolic Health Score (If you don't know these numbers, yet, that's ok. Keep moving through the book. You can come back to this later.)

1. ________ HDL-C
2. ________ Triglycerides
3. ________ Fasting Glucose
4. ________ Blood Pressure
5. ________ Waist

________ Total number in range (0-5, check Chapter 6 for ranges)

Plan when you'll reassess your metrics (monthly, quarterly, etc)

____

____

____

Your Mind Level is Set

You now have what most people lack: a reliable way to think about health decisions. You can assess where you are, filter new information through proven criteria, and approach your body as a trusted partner rather than an opponent.

This foundation prepares you for something that might surprise you. Most people expect the next step to be diet or exercise. But before you can fuel your body properly or build physical strength, there's a more fundamental system that needs attention.

Without this foundation working properly, even perfect nutrition and exercise plans fall short. It's why driven professionals like you can follow strict diets and intense workout routines yet still feel exhausted, gain weight, or struggle with cravings.

The missing piece? Recovery. Your body's ability to rest, repair, and reset each day.

With your Mind toolkit complete, you're ready to move to Level 2 of the Hierarchy of Wellth: Mend. Here, you'll learn how to pay off the sleep and stress debt that's been quietly undermining every other health effort you've made.

Mind Takeaways

1. **Your Why is Your Fuel:** Willpower is finite, but purpose endures through difficult moments.
2. **Use the Three-Check Decision Filter:** Does this solve an actual problem? Is there evidence it will work? Does it fit my real life?
3. **Shift from Opponent to Partner:** Stop fighting your body and start listening to it as a trusted ally.

4. **Your Health Balance Sheet:** Daily choices build assets or create liabilities that compound over time.
5. **You Can't Manage What You Don't Measure:** Health metrics provide the same confidence as financial tracking.
6. **Metrics are Tools, Not Judges:** Approach your numbers with curiosity, not judgment.

PART 2

MEND

"I live life at 211 degrees Fahrenheit. Almost boiling. There's no room for something to go wrong and no downtime."

Russ, a 49-year-old financial advisor, lives life with intensity. Despite exercising intensely every day, he had been steadily gaining weight for a decade. He slept just 4-5 hours a night, woke up naturally at 4 am with his mind racing, and never took breaks during his packed workday.

When we started working together, his breakthrough was actually the *opposite* of everything he'd been trying. He began to see that recovery isn't a luxury for high performers. It's what makes everything else possible.

Russ set a goal of getting 6 hours of sleep. When he woke at his usual 4 am, he began telling himself it wasn't time to get up yet and would practice the breathing techniques he'd learned.

To his surprise, he started falling back asleep. Within three months, Russ was consistently sleeping 6.5 hours per night. His weight dropped to its lowest "in a long time."

When we first assessed Russ, his Mend score was a 3. After focusing on sleep for a few months, his Mend score improved to a 6.

Russ's story reflects a pattern I see constantly with financial advisors. They approach health the way many people approach investing. They jump straight into aggressive actions, trying to outrun poor habits with intensity, much like trying to invest their way out of credit card debt.

High achievers like Russ are wired to push through, not slow down. I, too, spent years believing that rest was for other people who weren't as driven or didn't have as much responsibility. It took a health crisis to teach me that recovery goes hand-in-hand with long-term achievement.

But why is recovery so hard for people like us? The answer lies in understanding how our modern lifestyle creates challenges our bodies weren't designed to handle.

We Are Modern-Day Kings and Queens

You may not wear a crown, but in many ways, you live like royalty. We have access to comforts that even the wealthiest rulers in history couldn't imagine: food available 24/7, temperature-controlled environments, transportation without effort, entertainment on demand, and endless information at our fingertips.

We sit on our "thrones" (our desks, our couches, our conference calls) managing the pressures of modern life. While this lifestyle may look like success, there's a hidden cost.

Historically, ailments like gout, obesity, high blood pressure, heart disease, and anxiety were known as "diseases of kings." Not because kings were weak, but because they had abundance and leisure without the movement, natural rhythms, or physical demands their bodies were designed for.

Sound familiar?

Today, we're suffering from those same "royal diseases." They've become common in anyone with access to constant calories, chronic stress, minimal movement, disrupted sleep, and phones that never stop buzzing.

This modern lifestyle keeps many high achievers stuck at 4-6 scores, functioning but not thriving. Our physiology is ancient, but our culture is accelerating. And the tension between the two shows up in our bodies.

The real challenge of modern health is learning to reconcile our biology with our environment. We were built to move, rest, rise with the sun, and sleep in darkness. But our culture rewards convenience, sitting all day, snacking all night, living on autopilot.

I'm not here to condemn our culture. We live in a wonderful time in history in many ways. But I am here to let you know that recovery won't come as easily to us as it did to those in the past because of all the distractions and disruptions. So we will need to be aware of our situation and learn to live intentionally.

Recovery's Place in Your Hierarchy of Wellth

With your Mind level established through awareness and curiosity, you're ready for the second level: Mend. This recovery level creates the conditions for everything that follows.

The Hierarchy of Wellth™

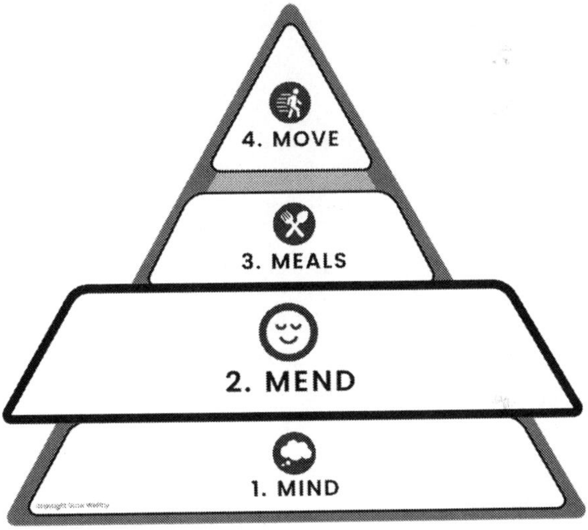

4. MOVE
3. MEALS
2. MEND
1. MIND

"Mend" is the second level of the Hierarchy of Wellth.

Mend practices are often the most neglected of the 4M's, so spending some time on this level is an easy way to get a higher score overall. Many people see their biggest improvements in this category first.

Consider your own recovery patterns right now. Do you prioritize sleep and manage stress effectively, or are you running on caffeine and adrenaline while telling yourself you'll "rest when things slow down"?

Without proper recovery, even perfect nutrition and exercise plans fall short. Russ's success wasn't because he pushed harder; it was because he rebuilt his recovery level first.

Recovery isn't optional in our modern world, so in the next chapter, you'll discover how to activate your body's built-in recovery systems and why most people unknowingly stay stuck in survival mode.

CHAPTER 6

Use Your Recovery Switch

Michael Kitces, a well-known voice in the financial advisory world, shared something fascinating when I was a guest on his podcast.

He'd been tracking his sleep for years and noticed a clear pattern. In months when he averaged just 30 minutes *more* sleep than usual, he lost weight without changing his workouts or diet. In months when he averaged 30 minutes *less*, he *gained* weight.

The difference wasn't a new exercise program or a diet overhaul. It was simply that his body had more time in *recovery mode.*

You can listen to our full conversation on the Financial Advisor Success Podcast, episode 366, by visiting this website www.growwellthy.com/kitces or scanning the QR code below.

Michael's observation points to an important truth: *your body already has a powerful, built-in recovery master operator. You just have to know how to work with it.*

The Body's Recovery Master Operator

That master operator is your nervous system. Specifically, the *parasympathetic branch* of your autonomic nervous system (ANS).

Think of your nervous system as the control tower for every other system in your body.

It has two main modes:

Sympathetic ("fight or flight") → your survival setting.

- Heart rate speeds up.
- Digestion and repair pause.
- Muscles tense for action.

Parasympathetic ("rest and digest") → your recovery setting.

- Heart rate slows down.
- Digestion improves.
- Cells repair and rebuild.

Your health depends on how much time you spend in recovery mode. And the fascinating thing? Daytime calm and nighttime deep sleep are not separate systems. They're both products of this same master operator.

The Switchboard Operator: Your Vagus Nerve

If the nervous system is the control tower, the *vagus nerve* is the switchboard operator.

When it senses safety, it sends a "green light" for other systems to initiate repair. For example:

- Immune system → repairs damaged tissue.
- Hormonal system → releases growth hormone, balances stress hormones.
- Digestive system → absorb and process nutrients.
- Brain → prepares for memory consolidation and emotional processing during sleep.

When it senses a threat, the vagus nerve sends a "red light" instead: stand down on repair; survival first.

The vagus nerve connects your brain to your major organs (heart, lungs, gut), and it can be *manually* activated. That means you don't have to wait for your environment to calm down before you do. You can flip the switch yourself.

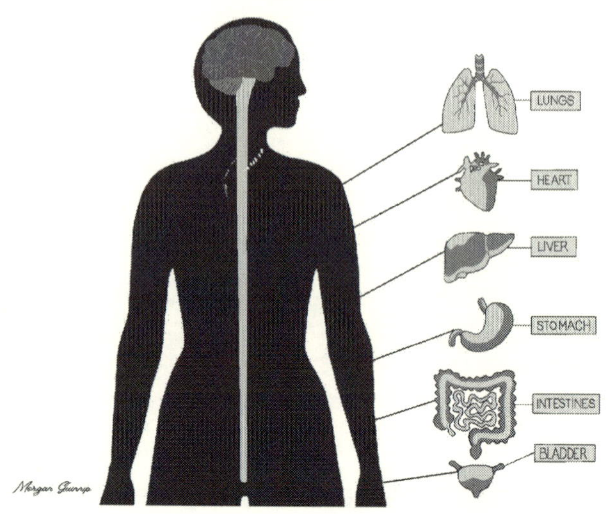

Your vagus nerve runs from the brain to the vital organs and regulates your stress response.

Signs You're Stuck in Survival Mode

When you ignore your body's signals, you stay stuck in sympathetic overdrive. That's exactly what happened to me.

Despite my training as an exercise physiologist, I treated my symptoms as random inconveniences instead of connected clues:

- Recurring ovarian cysts and painful cycles.
- Skin tags and heart palpitations after sugar.
- Stomach aches after meals, jaw tension, and sugar cravings.

- Energy crashes and dizzy spells from low iron and skipped meals.

Add in late nights, constant pressure, and a pride in "thriving under stress," and I was basically locking the switchboard in red-light mode 24/7.

When sepsis struck in Australia, it wasn't "out of nowhere." It was years of ignored warning signals from my body's recovery system.

Common signs that you might be stuck in survival mode include:

Physical symptoms:

- Trouble falling asleep or staying asleep
- Waking up tired despite sleeping
- Afternoon energy crashes that require caffeine
- Frequent colds or infections
- Digestive issues or stomach problems
- Tension headaches or jaw clenching
- Weight gain around the midsection

Mental and emotional signs:

- Feeling "wired but tired"
- Difficulty concentrating or brain fog

- Increased irritability or short temper
- Feeling overwhelmed by normal tasks
- Craving sugar or comfort foods
- Relying on caffeine to function
- Feeling anxious or restless even when sitting still

Have you trained yourself to ignore your body's signals that it needs more recovery? To power through discomfort, and to treat symptoms like interruptions instead of invitations?

Looking back, my Mend score was probably a 2 or 3. I was surviving on adrenaline and willpower instead of protecting my recovery time.

Start listening to your body and understanding what your signals really mean so you can break free from survival mode.

Daytime Recovery

While you are awake, you can tell your vagus nerve to flip that switch at any time.

Here are a few ways:

- **Box breathing:** Inhale for 4, hold for 4, exhale for 4, hold for 4.
- **Humming or singing:** Stimulates vagus activity through the vocal cords.

- **Laughing:** Signals safety to your nervous system.
- **Legs-up-the-wall:** Promotes calm and circulation.
- **Slow walks in nature:** Combines gentle movement with visual relaxation cues.

These aren't just "stress hacks". They prime your nervous system for more calm during the day and deeper sleep later that night.

But here's what these techniques can't fix: a calendar your nervous system can't afford.

These vagus nerve techniques help in the moment when stress hits. They're your emergency toolkit for acute stress responses. However, if you're chronically stressed, these tools are like bailing water from a boat while the faucet keeps running.

Chronic stress stems from a lifestyle mismatch. Your nervous system is telling you that your current commitments exceed your capacity. The solution requires looking at your calendar with the same rigor you'd apply to a client's overstretched budget.

Ask yourself:

- What commitments drain my energy without adding meaningful value?
- Which obligations am I keeping out of guilt rather than purpose?

- Where am I saying yes when I should be saying no?

No amount of breathing exercises will compensate for consistently working 70-hour weeks. No meditation practice can offset perpetual calendar overload. The vagus nerve techniques help you recover from necessary stress. Calendar culling prevents unnecessary stress from overwhelming your system in the first place.

Start by blocking recovery time on your calendar before adding new commitments. Protect your sleep window, meal times, and movement breaks as non-negotiable. Then evaluate each remaining commitment against your capacity. Some things will need to go.

Your nervous system operates on a budget, and chronic stress signals you're spending beyond your means. Once you right-size your calendar, those vagus nerve techniques become powerful tools for handling life's inevitable acute stressors.

Nighttime Recovery

When your switchboard operator spends most of the day flashing the green light, it's much easier to slip into the deep, restorative stages of sleep.

Most adults thrive somewhere between 7–9 hours of total sleep, but the real goal is to find *your* sweet spot, the amount that leaves you feeling alert, steady, and focused the next day.

If you're averaging 6 hours, don't worry about jumping straight to 8. Instead, nudge your average up by 15–30 minutes most nights. Small gains over time often bring bigger improvements than trying to overhaul your sleep in one leap.

What disrupts nighttime recovery:

Alcohol: While alcohol might help you fall asleep initially, it severely disrupts your sleep architecture. It blocks REM sleep and causes frequent wake-ups throughout the night. Even moderate drinking 2-3 hours before bed can impact sleep quality. Your liver works overtime to process alcohol when it should be focused on repair and restoration.

Late eating: Eating within 2-3 hours of bedtime keeps your digestive system active when it should be winding down. This elevates your core body temperature and keeps insulin levels high, both of which interfere with deep sleep. Your body can't focus on cellular repair when it's busy digesting food.

Quality matters as much as quantity:

Deep Sleep (slow-wave): Physical repair, growth hormone release, fat burning. Most of it happens in the first half of the night.

REM Sleep: Brain health, memory consolidation, emotional processing, stress hormone regulation. Most of it happens in the second half of the night.

Both stages are critical, and they depend on how your nervous system has been operating all day. You can't force quality sleep at night if your body has been stuck in survival mode from sunrise to bedtime. You have to earn it by managing your switchboard during the day. So when night comes, your body naturally shifts into its most restorative rhythms.

Other ways to improve your sleep quality: create a winddown routine, have a consistent bedtime, and keep your room dark and cool.

Why Recovery is So Important

Feeling rested is important, but it goes beyond that. Everything else in your body works better when your body is recovering well each day: decision-making, emotional resilience, metabolism, and performance.

Recovery mode:

- Improves mental clarity under pressure.
- Enhances your immune system.
- Regulates your appetite and weight.
- Boosts your energy without relying on caffeine.

Sometimes, just 30 extra minutes in recovery mode, whether during the day or in sleep, has a bigger impact on your health than hours in the gym or a strict diet plan.

Recovery isn't something that happens by accident in our modern world. It requires intentional choices throughout the day, starting with one of the most overlooked signals your body relies on to know when to rest and when to be alert. In the next chapter, you'll discover how to use light as a powerful tool to support your recovery system.

CHAPTER 7

Fix Your Light Diet

"You changed my life!"

That's the message Sean sent me after hearing me speak about how light affects sleep and stress.

He decided to make two changes: morning sunlight and turning off screens an hour before bed.

His sleep improved dramatically within a few days. Waking up refreshed made him feel less overwhelmed, and life got so much easier.

Remember how your body has a built-in recovery switch (your nervous system)? Light is the master control that programs when that switch turns on and off. Without proper light timing, you won't get the quality rest your body needs.

Fix your light diet, and you'll fall asleep faster, stay asleep longer, and wake up naturally refreshed - often within just a few days. This is why light is so important for paying off your health debt. You can't force quality sleep at night if your body doesn't know it's supposed to be sleepy.

Light: Your Master Conductor

Your body responds to light the same way it responds to food. Most of us are running on a "junk light" diet:

- Wake up in the dark
- Work under fluorescent lights
- Scroll through the evening
- Fall asleep with screens still glowing

That light overload messes with your sleep, hunger, mood, and metabolism - even if you're trying to eat well or move more.

Imagine your body as an orchestra. Every system represents different musicians. Light is your master conductor. For millennia, sunrise and sunset were the most reliable signals in our environment. Your brain uses these light patterns to orchestrate hormone production, body temperature, metabolism, and cognitive performance.

While feeding patterns and movement matter, light sets the tempo for everything else. When you get light right, the other rhythms often fall into place naturally.

This is why addressing light exposure can improve your scores across all four M's. Proper light timing enhances decision-making, sleep, nutrition, and movement.

We've Lost Our Dark Nights

We used to have dark nights. Now we have Netflix nights. And streetlight nights. And building light nights. And sidewalk-bright-as-day nights.

Since the 1950s, light pollution has exploded across America. In many places today, even the North Star is no longer visible. The glow that's blocking the stars is also disrupting your biology.

Why does this matter? Because your body needs darkness to repair.

A 2025 study of nearly 12,000 adults found that those exposed to more outdoor light at night had higher odds of diabetes, metabolic syndrome, obesity, and high cholesterol, even after controlling for income, location, and lifestyle.[20]

Light at night throws off your internal clock and messes with melatonin (sleepy hormone), cortisol (stress hormone), and insulin (food hormone) regulation. Your body doesn't know it's time to shut down and reset.

Building a Better Light Diet

If you have a junk light diet, it's easy to fix one sunrise, light break, or dim evening at a time.

Morning: Get outside within 30 minutes of waking. Five to ten minutes is enough. Use your naked eyes because sunglasses and windows block the light signals your brain needs to wake up and set your body clock.

Midday: Take a "light break" outside. This reinforces your circadian rhythm and boosts afternoon energy.

Evening: Watch the sunset with bare eyes. This natural dimming signals your body to start winding down. Dim the lights in your home after sunset. No overhead lights one hour before bed. Use lamps, red light bulbs, or salt lamps instead. Turn screens off or wear amber glasses. The dimmer your evenings, the more melatonin you make, the deeper you sleep, the better your blood sugar, and the fewer late-night cravings you'll have. Lots of wins with one simple light shift.

Night: Use blackout curtains to block streetlights. Cover electronic indicator lights. If you get up in the night to use the bathroom, use as little light as possible. Consider switching to red sensor night lights in your bathroom. You don't have to go full cave mode. Just dial it down.

Light is free, easy, and works immediately. Every light choice nudges your body back into rhythm, making everything else easier.

Living in a Natural Rhythm

I've seen this natural light rhythm in action while living in Portugal. They aren't following complicated health programs. They simply live in harmony with light patterns we've forgotten.

Morning light naturally brings them outdoors. Midday brightness invites afternoon rest. Cool evenings draw them back to community. As darkness falls, they wind down without screens or artificial lights. Their bodies follow the same light cues yours are designed for.

You don't need to move to Portugal to access this wisdom. These same natural rhythms exist within your body right now, waiting to be rediscovered.

In the next chapter, I put together a Mend Toolkit so you can start working on improving your own natural rhythm.

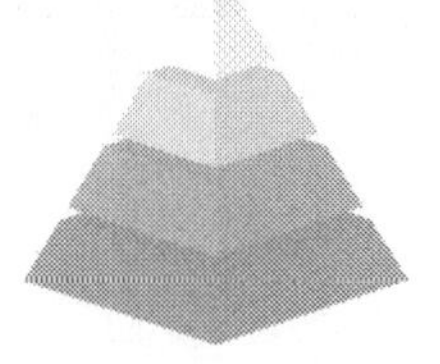

CHAPTER 8

Mend Toolkit

There was a point when I was writing this book that I realized I wouldn't make my deadline. I faced a choice: push myself to exhaustion or honor my wellbeing.

Ten years ago, I would have sacrificed my health to meet that date. Staying up all night, working frantically, my identity tied to being perfect no matter the cost. That's the same mindset that led to my sepsis and emergency surgery in Australia.

But I've learned there's usually no real fire. No reason to "put the noose around my own neck," as my husband wisely said.

Each time I had to choose between pushing harder or being sustainable, I chose the latter. Not because I was giving up or being lazy, but because I was respecting my body, setting boundaries that protect my health, and modeling the very principles I teach.

This is what applying the Mend level looks like in real life. It's recognizing when old patterns try to resurface and making intentional choices that support your long-term wellbeing instead of short-term pressure.

Your Mend Assessment

Rate your MEND health by scoring yourself on four questions:

Health Continuum

Rate Your Health on this Scale of 1-10.

Struggling | Inconsistent | Strong

0 1 2 3 4 5 6 7 8 9 10

1. ______ **How restorative is your sleep quantity and quality?**

1-3 = Less than 6 hours, poor quality, wake up tired

4-6 = 6-7 hours, inconsistent quality, sometimes refreshed

7-9 = 7-8 hours, good quality, usually wake refreshed

10 = 7-9 hours, excellent quality, always wake energized

2. ______ **How well do you manage stress throughout the day?**

1-3 = Constantly overwhelmed, no stress management tools

4-6 = Often stressed, occasional use of calming techniques

7-9 = Generally manage stress well, regular recovery practices

10 = Excellent stress resilience, automatic recovery responses

3. _____ **How stable is your energy throughout the day?**

1-3 = Major crashes, depend on caffeine, exhausted evenings

4-6 = Some ups and downs, moderate caffeine dependence

7-9 = Generally steady energy, minimal caffeine needs

10 = Consistent high energy, no artificial stimulants needed

4. _____ **How well do you manage your light exposure and circadian rhythm?**

1-3 = Poor light habits, disrupted sleep-wake cycle

4-6 = Some awareness of light impact, inconsistent habits

7-9 = Good light hygiene, mostly aligned with natural rhythms

10 = Optimized light exposure, perfect circadian alignment

_____ Total / 4 = _______ MEND Score

Your Recovery Action Plan

Choose your priority recovery practice:

- Protect your sleep window
    - Stop eating 2-3 hours before bed
    - Create a consistent bedtime routine
    - Keep the bedroom cool and dark
- Activate your recovery switch daily
    - Box breathing between stressful moments

  - Try legs-up-the-wall pose
  - Take a slow walk in nature

- **Fix your light diet**
  - Get morning sunlight within 30 minutes of waking
  - Dim lights after sunset
  - Minimize screens the hour before bed

Your Mend Level is Set

Remember Russ, who lived at "211 degrees"? His transformation came when he realized he'd been living beyond his energy means. By treating sleep as an essential bill that had to be paid, he dropped weight and gained energy.

You now have practical tools to pay your recovery bills consistently. With this Mend level in place, you're ready for Level 3: Meals. This is where you will learn to fuel your body based on the strong recovery infrastructure you've built.

Here's why this sequence matters: when your nervous system is stuck in survival mode, your body hoards calories and craves quick energy. But when your recovery systems work properly, your body can actually use the nutrition you provide. It stops fighting against your food choices and starts working with them.

Those who see the biggest transformations don't just eat better. Their bodies are primed to use that nutrition effectively. That's the power of building health in the right order.

Mend Takeaways

1. **Recovery Isn't Optional in Modern Life:** Unlike our ancestors, we must intentionally create recovery because our environment constantly disrupts our natural rhythms with artificial light, chronic stress, and endless distractions.

2. **Your Foundation Determines Everything:** You can't build lasting health by pushing harder. Recovery creates the biological base that makes nutrition and movement practices actually work.

3. **Vagus Nerve = Your Recovery Switch:** You can manually activate your parasympathetic nervous system through simple techniques like breathing, humming, or legs-up-the-wall.

4. **Daytime Recovery Drives Nighttime Quality:** The calmer you are during the day, the deeper and more restorative your sleep will be.

5. **Light is Your Master Conductor:** Light sets the tempo for your entire biological orchestra. When you get light right, other rhythms often fall into place naturally.

6. **Build a Better Light Diet:** Morning light through naked eyes, midday light breaks, sunset watching, and dimmed evening lights. Every light choice nudges your body back into rhythm.

PART 3

MEALS

Heidi had always been "that friend" who could eat anything without gaining weight. For five decades, her body simply cooperated.

Then everything changed.

Around her 50th birthday, the pounds started creeping on. By 61, when we first met, she'd gained 40 pounds. "It's just menopause," she told me, resigned to what seemed inevitable.

Heidi had tried everything: cutting calories, eliminating carbs, following the latest diet trends. Nothing worked. She felt defeated.

When we first assessed Heidi, her overall score was a 4, including her Meals score. Despite trying to eat healthy, she didn't have a good framework of what and when to eat. With her frequent travel, late meals and drinks, she was staying in health debt.

When she joined one of my small groups as a last resort, Heidi started tracking her food not to restrict it, but to understand it.

The insight was immediate: her nutrition wasn't balanced. Too many low-fiber carbs, not enough protein, and most calories consumed late in the day.

After learning to smarten up her carbs with fiber, get protein at every meal, and redistribute calories earlier in the day, her body responded quickly. Within three months, she'd lost 23 pounds.

"All my pants are baggy, and I'm beginning to recognize myself in the mirror!"

After a year: 48 pounds lost, 6 inches off her waist, and all her "red" numbers turned "green." Most importantly, she never felt deprived. Her Meals score had jumped from a 4 to an 8, which helped pull her overall score up to a 7.

The diet industry conditions us to think about nutrition in terms of restriction and willpower. But what if we focused on balance and nourishment instead?

Instead of asking "What foods should I eliminate?" Heidi started asking, "*What* nutrients does my body need and *when* does it need them?"

Nutrition's Place in Your Hierarchy of Wellth

With your Mind and Mend levels in place, you're ready for the third level: Meals.

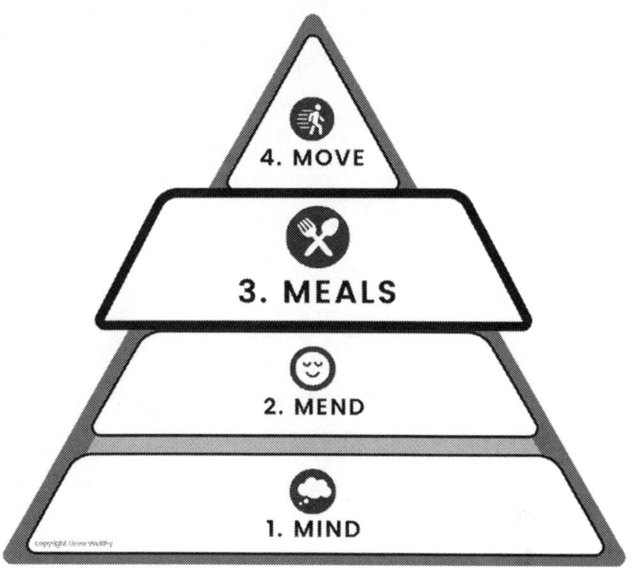

"Meals" is the third level of the Hierarchy of Wellth.

This sequence matters. When your recovery systems function properly, your body can actually use the nutrition you provide. Heidi's success came from this integrated approach. Her improved Mind and Mend scores allowed her Meals transformation to take hold and create significant, lasting results.

Think about your current eating patterns. Do you have a systematic approach to nutrition, or do you find yourself cycling between restriction and overeating, or following fads without understanding what you should really be doing?

Meals practices are *powerful.* This is where my clients find clarity and confidence in their food choices. They start to feel peace from nagging cravings and can quickly climb even higher on the health score. But their ability to make big improvements happens when their food builds on solid recovery habits. Better food choices are easier to make when you are well rested.

The key to sustainable nutrition has less to do with willpower or restriction and more to do with understanding how your body manages energy. In the next chapter, you'll discover the two critical systems that determine whether you feel satisfied or constantly hungry, no matter what you eat.

CHAPTER 9

What Your Body Needs to Thrive

Annie would eat breakfast and be hungry again in two hours. Every morning: two eggs and toast. By 10 AM, she was reaching for snacks.

"I don't understand why I'm always hungry," she told me. "I eat breakfast, but I can't make it to lunch without grazing."

It wasn't that Annie was lacking willpower. Instead, her breakfast wasn't giving her body what it needed. Those eggs and toast didn't have enough protein or fiber to sustain her. Her blood sugar would spike from the toast, then crash, leaving her searching for more food.

When we balanced her breakfast with the right nutrients, everything changed. Suddenly, Annie could go 3-5 hours between meals without thinking about food. Her energy stayed steady all day, and she no longer needed an afternoon nap. To her delight, she dropped from 184 to 145 pounds in the following months.

Annie's breakthrough came from understanding two key systems that manage energy in your body: blood sugar regulation and metabolic flexibility.

When these systems work well together, your health improves. When they're struggling, you stay stuck no matter how much willpower you try to muster up.

Blood Sugar Regulation

Your blood sugar is like the speedometer in your car. When it's stable, you cruise smoothly through your day with steady energy. When it swings wildly, you experience metabolic stop-and-go traffic.

Each time you eat, your blood sugar rises. How much it rises and how quickly it returns to baseline determines whether you feel energized and satisfied or hungry and tired an hour later.

Healthy blood sugar patterns create gentle rises after meals, followed by gradual returns to baseline. Your energy stays steady and hunger signals work properly.

Problematic blood sugar patterns create sharp spikes followed by crashes. When blood sugar climbs too high too fast, your pancreas floods your system with insulin to bring it down quickly. This often overcorrects, sending blood sugar plummeting and triggering intense cravings for quick energy.

Over time, these repeated roller coaster rides can lead to insulin resistance, weight gain, and constant hunger.

The key is choosing foods and meal combinations that create gentle, sustained blood sugar responses rather than dramatic spikes and crashes.

Blood sugar stability is only half the equation. The other half is your body's ability to efficiently switch between different fuel sources.

Metabolic Flexibility

Your body has two primary fuel sources: glucose and fat. Healthy bodies switch between both efficiently.

Glucose comes from eating carbohydrates. It's readily available for immediate energy. Think of glucose as cash in your pocket.

Your body can also store glucose in your muscles and liver as glycogen to use later. Glycogen is like money in your checking account. It's available but requires a few extra steps to access.

Fat comes from eating fatty foods or from storing extra energy as fat. It's your most sustainable energy source. Think of fat like money in your savings account. It's accessible, but harder to get to.

Your Liver: The Captain of Your Metabolic Ship

Picture two people in a leaky rowboat. One is young and strong with a big bucket. As water seeps in, he bails quickly, keeping the boat afloat.

The other works just as hard but only has a spoon. Despite his effort, water accumulates and the boat begins to sink.

This is the difference between a healthy liver and a sluggish one.

A healthy liver (bucket) vs. a sluggish liver (spoon): both work hard, but only one can keep your metabolic boat afloat.

Your liver acts like your body's energy manager. It stores and releases glucose to keep your blood sugar steady, and it determines how easily you can access your stored fat for fuel. When your liver gets overwhelmed by too much sugar, processed foods, or chronic stress, it operates like the man with the spoon, working hard but unable to keep up with demand.

When I refer to a "sluggish" or "unhealthy" liver, I'm often talking about NAFLD (Non-Alcoholic Fatty Liver Disease). One in three people have this condition, yet most don't know it.[22]

When your liver becomes overwhelmed, it begins storing fat within itself, like water accumulating in that leaky boat. This fatty buildup impairs the liver's ability to manage your energy systems efficiently.

Annie's constant hunger and lagging afternoon energy was a sign her liver was struggling. When we reduced her sugar load and supported her liver health, her body regained its ability to switch between fuel sources efficiently.

Metabolic flexibility is your body's ability to switch between these fuel sources based on availability and need. Annie's body had grown dependent on quick glucose, creating constant carbohydrate cravings.

When she learned to balance her meals, her body rediscovered its ability to use stored fat between meals. This is why she could suddenly go 3-5 hours without eating and feel fine.

Your Energy Systems Work Together

Annie's transformation addressed both systems simultaneously. Balanced meals stabilized her blood sugar and restored her metabolic flexibility. Her body remembered how to use stored energy efficiently.

This explains why some people feel satisfied for hours after eating while others need constant snacks. Understanding these systems is what separates people scoring 7-10 from those stuck at 4-6.

You can stop beating yourself up for not having enough willpower. All you need is to support your systems so they work efficiently.

Now that you understand how your body manages energy, let's explore exactly what to eat to support these systems.

CHAPTER 10

What to Eat

Carl had been a CFP® for three decades, helping clients build balanced portfolios and secure financial futures. But when it came to his own health, this analytical southern gentleman was struggling.

His doctor delivered an ultimatum: get your A1C down from 6.5, or start taking metformin for diabetes. Carl loved his sweet tea and never met a dessert he didn't like. The idea of giving up these pleasures felt impossible.

"I've tried cutting carbs before," Carl told me during our first conversation. "But I always end up right back where I started. I don't understand why I can't stick with it."

When we assessed Carl, his Meals score was a concerning 2. He understood the importance of nutrition, but lacked a framework that made sense to his analytical mind.

Carl's struggle had nothing to do with willpower. Like many of us, he was unknowingly consuming foods that were working against his body's natural systems.

What to Minimize: Food Taxes

Beyond just eating "healthy," the quality of your food matters. Some foods act like "taxes" on your health, requiring your body to spend energy on damage control rather than growth and repair.

Remember the boat analogy from the previous chapter? Some foods actively "punch holes in your boat," forcing your liver and other organs to work overtime.

These taxes on your body create something researchers call "inflammaging" (aging quicker from inflammation). Chronic inflammation isn't a normal part of aging. It's a byproduct of our modern environment. Studies comparing industrialized populations to indigenous communities found that only those in industrialized settings showed a rise in inflammation with age.[21]

Major Food Taxes Include:

Alcohol: Alcohol is socially acceptable, even expected, at many client dinners and industry events, but the biological cost is high. The World Health Organization classifies alcohol as a carcinogen, and even moderate drinking places a significant burden on your liver.[28,29]

Excess Sugar: Too much sugar causes blood glucose spikes, too much insulin, and an overwhelmed liver. This can lead to diabetes and fatty liver disease.

Ultra-Processed Foods: These foods (such as chips, hot dogs, etc) contain industrial oils, artificial additives, and preservatives that create inflammation and tax your body. They provide calories without nutrients while requiring extra energy to process.

This is why Carl needed more than another diet. He needed a framework that would support his body's energy systems rather than tax them. That's where the Smart CFP approach comes in.

The Smart CFP Approach

The Smart CFP approach gives you a systematic way to fuel your body while minimizing these food taxes.

In finance, CFP® stands for Certified Financial Planner™. In nutrition, I use CFP to represent the building blocks of food: **Carbs, Fats, and Proteins.**

Understanding how to balance these macronutrients (macros) supports the energy systems we discussed in the previous chapter.

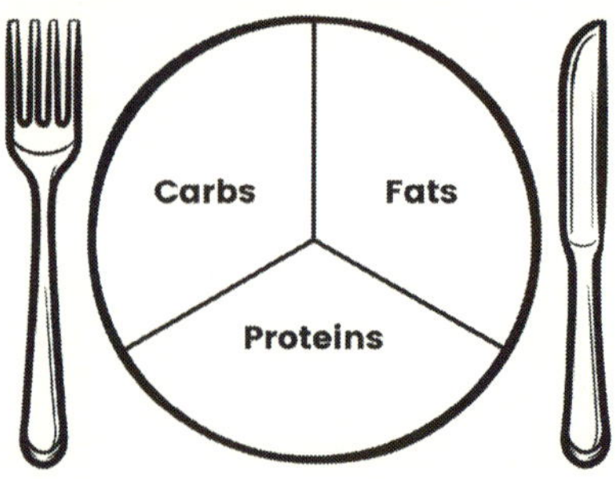

Balanced carbohydrates, fats, and proteins make up the CFP's of nutrition.

C = Smart Carbohydrates

Carbs aren't "bad" - quality, quantity, and timing matter. The key distinction is between Smart Carbs and Simple Carbs.

Smart Carbs have a 5:1 carb-to-fiber ratio (at least 1 gram of fiber for every 5 grams of carbs). The fiber slows digestion and stabilizes blood sugar.

Simple Carbs have poor ratios (i.e. 10:1), causing blood sugar spikes and energy crashes.

Check this ratio on nutrition labels: divide total carbs by fiber grams.

Examples:

- White bread: 30g carbs, 2g fiber = 15:1 ratio (Simple)
- High-fiber bread: 25g carbs, 5g fiber = 5:1 ratio (Smart)

- Pear: 20g carbs, 5g fiber = 4:1 ratio (Smart)
- Watermelon: 15g carbs, 1g fiber = 15:1 ratio (Simple)

Simple swaps like berries instead of melon or whole-grain bread instead of white can stabilize blood sugar and reduce cravings.

F = Fats

Fats support hormone production, brain health, and provide sustainable fuel. Focus on real food sources: olive oil, avocados, nuts, and omega-3-rich fish.

Watch portion sizes. Fat has over twice the calories per gram as carbs or protein. Hidden fats in restaurant meals and high-calorie foods like cheese and nuts can add up quickly.

P = Proteins

Protein builds and repairs tissues, creates enzymes, and supports immune function. Without enough, your body breaks down muscle tissue.

Aim for protein at every meal. Most people eat too many carbs and fats, but not enough protein.

The Balanced Plate

Use your hand as a measuring tool:

- **Protein:** 1-2 palm-sized portions

- **Non-starchy vegetables:** 2-3 fist-sized portions
- **Healthy fats:** 1-2 thumb-sized portions
- **Smart Carbs:** 1-2 cupped handfuls

The Balanced Plate

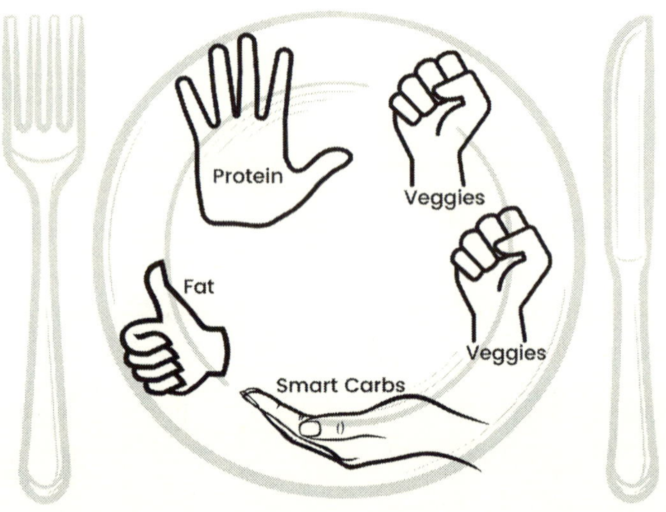

Visualize your serving sizes by using your hand as a guide.

General targets for most adults:

- Protein: 25-40g per meal
- Smart Carbs: 40-60g per meal (following the 5:1 principle)
- Healthy Fats: 15-25g per meal

Keep in mind that your unique situation may require modifications to your macro balance.

Create Your Go-To Meals

Develop 6-12 meals you enjoy and can easily assemble: 2-4 breakfasts, lunches, and dinners to rotate throughout the week. This prevents decision fatigue and eliminates the scramble for takeout when you're exhausted. I added a 5-day meal plan to the the Grow Wellthy Resource Hub linked at the beginning and end of this book.

Carl's Transformation

"Think of your daily food intake as having three main components: carbs, fats, and proteins," I explained to Carl. "Each serves a purpose, but going too heavy in one area while ignoring others creates problems."

Carl's eyes lit up. "So you're saying I'm eating too many carbs and not enough protein?"

Exactly. He started tracking his food intake, asking himself: "Does this dessert fit with how balanced my eating has been today?"

For the first time, nutrition felt logical rather than restrictive. Three months later, his A1C had dropped significantly. Carl sent me a heartfelt note saying I had "saved his life," perhaps dramatic, but his relief was genuine.

When you minimize food taxes while balancing your CFPs, you create optimal conditions for improving your health score and staying healthy.

CHAPTER 11

When & How to Eat

Remember Heidi from earlier? She had mastered the "what to eat" part of her transformation by balancing her CFPs, choosing Smart Carbs, and building go-to meals. But she was struggling with one pattern that kept sabotaging her progress.

"I eat well all day," she told me during one of our group calls. "But by dinner, I'm starving. I end up eating my biggest meal late in the day."

Sound familiar? Heidi was following the most common eating pattern in America: minimal breakfast, light lunch, then backloading most calories into the evening hours.

When we analyzed her eating schedule, most of her calories were in the second half of the day. This late eating was keeping her body in glucose-burning mode when it should have been switching to fat-burning for overnight repair.

The solution wasn't complicated, but it required a mindset shift. Instead of saving her appetite for dinner, Heidi learned to redistribute her calories earlier in the day. She started eating a substantial breakfast with protein, a satisfying lunch, and a lighter dinner. Most importantly, she "closed her kitchen" by 7 PM.

"The first couple of weeks felt weird," Heidi admitted. "But pretty soon, I wasn't even that hungry for dinner." Her sleep and energy improved, and she started eating her last meal even earlier because it felt so good.

This timing adjustment became the final piece of Heidi's transformation puzzle. Combined with her improved food choices, the strategic timing helped move her Meals score from 4 to 8.

Feeding and Fasting Windows

One of the most powerful ways to support metabolic health is by defining your feeding and fasting windows.

A **feeding window** is when you consume your food each day.

A **fasting window** is when you stop eating, allowing your body to rest, repair, and shift into fat-burning mode.

Most people unknowingly stretch their feeding window across 14-16 hours, starting with early morning bites and ending with late evening snacks.

Research suggests a better approach: consolidate eating to 10-12 hours and close the kitchen 2-3 hours before bedtime. This might mean eating from 8 AM to 8 PM.

During fasting windows, insulin levels drop, helping your body access stored fat, reduce inflammation, and reset hunger hormones. This supports brain function, hormone regulation, and metabolic health beyond simple calorie control.

Calorie Shapes

The timing of your calories forms a shape that affects your health:

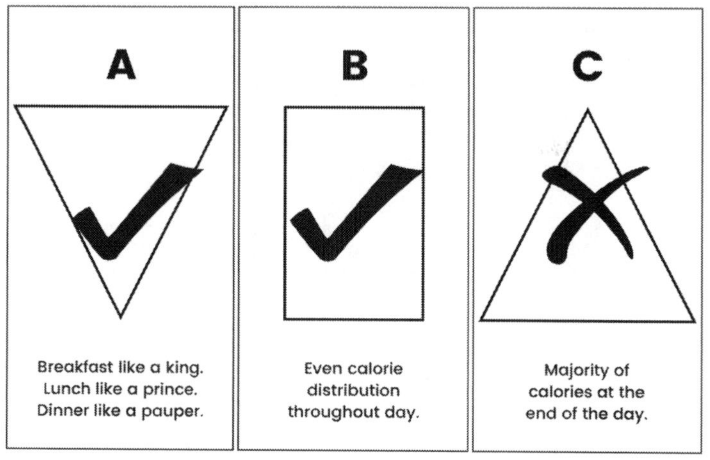

How you allocate your calories throughout the day has an impact on your health.

Shape A: Most calories at breakfast, tapering to dinner (upside-down triangle) ✓

Shape B: Evenly distributed calories across meals (rectangle) ✓

Shape C: Few calories early, heavy eating at night (triangle) ✗

Most people fall into Shape C, skipping breakfast, powering through the day, then backloading calories into dinner and evening snacks.

"But what if I'm not hungry for breakfast?"

If you're not hungry in the morning, that's a sign your metabolism has adapted to Shape C eating. Don't force food when you're not hungry. Instead, wait until you feel genuinely hungry, then make that first meal substantial and balanced with protein, smart carbs, and healthy fats.

Over time, as you eat more in the first half of the day and less at night, your hunger patterns will shift. Your body will start expecting fuel earlier and needing less food in the evening. This metabolic adjustment usually takes 2-3 weeks of consistent timing.

Shape C costs:

- Weight gain and reduced overnight fat burning
- Disrupted blood sugar and insulin balance
- Poor sleep quality

Better strategy: Choose Shape A (ideal) or B. Reallocate some evening food earlier in the day. The human body thrives when digestion winds down before sleep.

Eat More, Less Often (EMLO)

Eating a few larger meals, including a balance of all three macronutrients (CFPs), supports metabolic flexibility better than grazing all day. This helps your body feel satisfied and go 3-5 hours between meals. Remember Annie? That's what she did. EMLO gives your body time to tap into fat stores between meals and prevents energy crashes that lead to cravings.

Mindful Eating Practices

Beyond *what* you eat and *when* you eat, *how* you eat matters:

HALT Check: Before eating, ask if you're truly Hungry, or perhaps Angry/Anxious, Lonely, or Tired.

Slow Down: Eat without screens, chew thoroughly, and stop when satisfied, not stuffed.

Food Order: Start with vegetables, then protein and fats, saving carbohydrates for last. This sequence stabilizes blood sugar.

Social Situations: Your Make-or-Break Moments

Let's be honest. Financial advisors have incredibly social careers. Client dinners, industry conferences, networking events, weekend retreats. Your calendar is packed with situations where food and drinks are central to relationship building.

This is where most health journeys derail. Not because you lack willpower, but because you're trying to navigate complex social dynamics while maintaining professional relationships.

Harris initially worried he'd have to become "that guy" who orders plain grilled chicken at every client dinner. Russ thought he'd miss out on the camaraderie of networking at conferences. Annie feared she'd lose the joy of spending the day at the lake with friends.

But here's what they discovered: you don't have to choose between your health and your social life. You just need a plan.

The Reality Check: These situations will happen 2-3 times per week for most advisors. If you don't have a plan, you'll default to whatever's easiest in the moment.

Client Dinners

The pressure here is real. You're building relationships while the wine list comes out and appetizers keep arriving.

Harris's strategy: "I started ordering club soda with lime first thing. It looks like a cocktail, keeps my hands busy, and nobody questions it. I'd scan the menu for the best protein option, then ask for vegetables instead of the potato. Most restaurants are happy to accommodate."

The key insight: your clients care more about the conversation than what's on your plate. Focus on them, not the bread basket.

Conferences

Three days of vendor lunches, evening receptions, and hospitality suites. It's a nutritional obstacle course.

Russ' approach: "I packed protein bars and ate one before every event so I wasn't making decisions while starving. At buffets, I'd walk the entire table first to see all options before filling my plate. Game changer."

Pro tip: Position yourself away from the food stations. You're there to network, not graze.

Travel

These are often the hardest because they're personal, not professional. Nobody wants to be the person who ruins the fun.

Annie's solution: "I'd volunteer to bring something healthy that I knew I'd enjoy, like a great salad or veggie tray. That way, I always had good options without making anyone else change their plans."

The magic happens when you realize you can fully participate in the experience without participating in every single food and drink offered. Harris, Russ, and Annie all learned the same lesson: preparation and intention, not deprivation.

They didn't become antisocial. They still attended events, built strong relationships, and enjoyed themselves while making conscious choices rather than defaulting to whatever appeared in front of them.

People who consistently apply these timing and social strategies often see their Meals scores move to 7-10. This is where healthy choices feel natural rather than forced.

CHAPTER 12

Meals Toolkit

You now understand how your body manages energy, what nutrients it needs, and when to fuel it strategically. Let's transform these concepts into daily habits you can sustain.

Heidi's transformation didn't happen because she found the perfect diet. It happened because she learned to work with her body's energy systems instead of against them. She stopped fighting food and started partnering with it.

When you balance your CFPs (Carbs, Fats, Proteins), time your feeding windows, and eat mindfully, food becomes fuel rather than a source of stress. You can stop wondering if you're doing it right and start feeling confident in your choices.

Your Meals Assessment

Rate your MEALS health by scoring yourself on four questions:

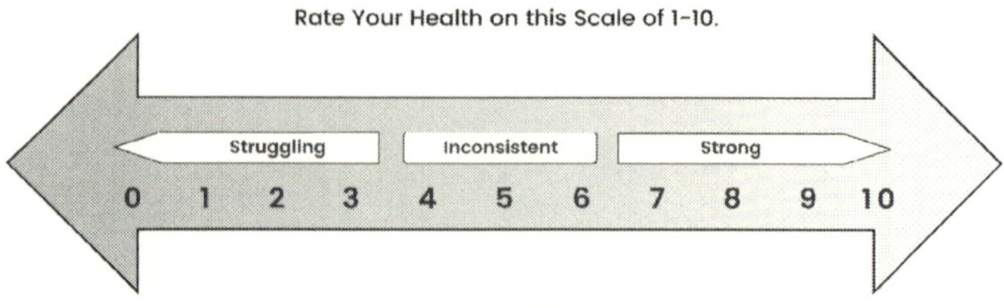

1. ______ **How well do you balance your nutrition?**

1-3 = Poor CFP balance, frequent processed foods, often dehydrated

4-6 = Inconsistent balance, some Smart Carbs, moderate hydration

7-9 = Generally balanced CFPs, mostly whole foods, well hydrated

10 = Optimal macro balance, precision nutrition, perfect hydration

2. ______ **How strategic is your meal timing?**

1-3 = Irregular eating, long feeding windows, late-night eating

4-6 = Somewhat regular meals, unclear about optimal timing

7-9 = Consistent timing, appropriate feeding/fasting windows

10 = Perfect timing, optimized calorie distribution throughout day

3. ______ **How mindful are your eating habits?**

1-3 = Emotional eating, always distracted meals, eat too fast

4-6 = Sometimes mindful, often eating while working or stressed

7-9 = Generally present while eating, good hunger/fullness awareness

10 = Completely intuitive eating, perfect mind-body connection

4. _____ **How well do you handle cravings and food taxes?**

1-3 = Frequent cravings, regular alcohol/sugar, late-night snacking

4-6 = Moderate cravings, occasional indulgences, some control

7-9 = Rare cravings, food taxes only on special occasions

10 = No cravings, complete freedom from food taxes

_____ Total / 4 = _______ MEALS Score

Your Nutrition Action Plan

Track and optimize your food:

Log your food for one week to understand your current patterns

- Check to see if your CFPs are balanced at each meal
- Calculate your carb-to-fiber ratios (aim for 5:1 or better)
- Identify your current Calorie Shape (A, B, or C):

Set your feeding window (aim for 12 hours or less): _____

Create your go-to meal rotation

- Download the 5-day meal plan from the Resource Hub, or

- Build your own Smart CFP combinations you actually enjoy

Practice mindful eating techniques

- Use HALT to check before eating (Hungry vs. Angry/Lonely/Tired)
- Slow down and minimize distractions while eating
- Try the food order: vegetables first, then protein and fats, carbs last

Your Meals Level is Set

You now have a systematic approach that works with your body's natural energy systems. By learning to balance your food budget (allocating the right nutrients at the right times), you're creating sustained energy, a stable mood, and long-term metabolic health.

Remember Harris, Kevin, and Heidi? Their transformations came from consistently applying these principles while maintaining their social and professional lives. You don't need perfection - you need strategy.

With your nutrition foundation in place, you're ready for the final level of the Hierarchy of Wellth: Move. You'll learn how to invest in physical fitness that builds on everything you've established.

Here's the crucial difference: when your Mind is focused, your Mend practices are restoring your energy, and your Meals are fueling your body efficiently, movement becomes what it's meant to be, an investment in your future strength and independence, not a desperate attempt to outrun poor habits.

You're no longer trying to exercise your way out of exhaustion or poor nutrition. You're building physical resilience on top of a body that's already functioning well.

Meals Takeaways

1. **Focus on Balance, Not Restriction:** Instead of asking "What should I eliminate?" ask "What nutrients does my body need and when does it need them?" This shift from deprivation to nourishment creates sustainable results.

2. **Your Liver is Your Metabolic Captain:** When overwhelmed by sugar and stress, your liver operates with a "spoon" instead of a "bucket," struggling to manage your body's energy systems efficiently.

3. **Smart CFP Approach:** Balance Smart Carbs (5:1 fiber ratio), Fats, and Proteins to support stable blood sugar and metabolic flexibility.

4. **Front-Load Calories:** Choose Shape A or B - eat more earlier in the day to reduce cravings, improve sleep, and manage weight.

5. **Mindful Eating:** Use HALT check, slow down, and eat vegetables first to improve satiety and blood sugar.

6. **Social Success:** Preparation and conscious choices allow you to maintain balance in any situation.

PART 4

MOVE: INVEST IN MUSCLE & FUNCTION

Mark, a high-performing advisor in his early 60s, walked into the locker room dripping with sweat. He'd just dominated the weight room with guys half his age, just like he'd been doing for the past three years.

He enjoyed it. Trainers praised him. Guys in their 30s were in awe. He could lift, drill, and plank with the best of them.

Yet when he stepped on the scale, his weight never went down. In fact, it had been on an upward trend for a while now. His pants weren't fitting, his cholesterol was rising, and his energy was tanking by midday.

"I don't get it," he told his wife over coffee. "I'm working out harder than anyone else my age. My trainer keeps pushing me to do more, but I feel worse every week."

Mark was trapped in the classic "more is better" mindset. Longer workouts. Higher intensity. Push through the joint pain. If the scale wasn't moving, he obviously wasn't working hard enough.

But Mark was making a fundamental mistake: treating exercise like a desperate transaction instead of a strategic investment. He was trying to punish his body into submission; a risky approach with a high probability of injury or burnout.

When we first assessed Mark, his Move score was an 8, with solid consistency and intensity. But his other 4M levels were struggling, pulling his overall score down to a 5 and creating an imbalanced approach that was working against him.

He had invested too heavily in intense exercise, thinking he could outrun his other habits. That approach may have worked when he was younger, but it had become a losing equation.

His approach was actually creating more stress, inflammation, and overeating, rather than building health that would carry him into his 70s.

Mark's breakthrough came when he realized he'd been approaching exercise like day-trading instead of retirement planning. He was chasing short-term results with unsustainable intensity.

His path forward had to include two things: diversifying his movement portfolio with low-level daily walks (not runs), rest days for muscle repair, and mobility work for joint health, while also working on the other 4M levels.

It felt weird to dial back his exercise at first, but within six months, Mark was fitter, pain-free, and 25 pounds lighter. More importantly, he was building the physical runway for a long, active retirement. His Move score improved a little, but his other 4M scores went up, pulling his overall score to a 7.

Movement's Place in Your Hierarchy of Wellth

You've now reached the fourth and final level of the Hierarchy of Wellth. This is where you build the strength and mobility that supports the life you want to live, both now and decades from now.

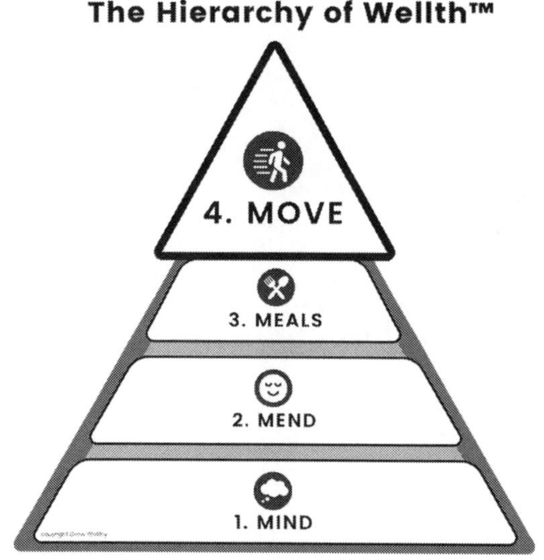

"Meals" is the fourth and final level of the Hierarchy of Wellth.

Movement comes last because without proper mindset, recovery, and nutrition, exercise often creates more problems than solutions, as Mark's story showed us. But when you build your movement on top of a strong foundation, it becomes a powerful multiplier of everything you've already established.

Consider your current relationship with movement. Do you have all your bases covered so you can keep doing all the things you love for decades to come? Or do you find yourself either avoiding exercise entirely or pushing through pain without a clear plan?

Movement has long been mistaken as a way to burn calories or punishment for 'bad' food choices. But it offers so much more than that. Movement gives you a body that functions well so you can live the life you want, both now and in retirement. Think of it as your growth investment in future mobility, strength, and independence.

Mark's story shows how even dedicated exercisers can get trapped in routines that work against them. The path to knowing how to move involves clearing away misconceptions. In the next two chapters, you'll discover the four exercise myths that keep high achievers stuck and what to do instead.

CHAPTER 13

Exercise Myths That Keep You Stuck (Part 1)

Carolyn stepped off the Peloton, sweat soaking her hair, gasping for air. Another grueling high-intensity ride in the books. At 54, she'd been grinding through cardio sessions for years, running, rowing, spinning, convinced that if she wasn't dying of exhaustion, she wasn't working hard enough.

Yet despite her dedication, the scale kept creeping upward. From 145 to 150 to 155 pounds. Each year brought another few pounds, and with menopause approaching, Carolyn was terrified it would only get worse.

"I don't understand," she told me during our first conversation. "I'm doing everything I'm supposed to do. I work out harder than anyone I know, but I keep gaining weight."

When we first assessed Carolyn, her Move score was a 5, lots of activity, but missing pieces and limited effectiveness.

Carolyn was trapped in the "cardio is everything" myth. She believed that sweating buckets and pushing her heart rate to the max was the only way to lose weight. But her relentless cardio routine was actually working against her, creating chronic stress that elevated cortisol and made fat loss nearly impossible (especially for the peri-menopausal stage of life).

When I explained that an effective movement routine has four components, not just cardiovascular endurance, Carolyn was skeptical. "If I add strength training, won't I just gain muscle weight? And if I do less cardio, won't I gain even more fat?"

But Carolyn was willing to try. She cut back her soul-crushing cardio sessions and added strength training three days a week. Combined with better recovery and balanced meals, her body's stress response dropped dramatically.

The results surprised even her. Not only did she lose the 10 pounds she'd been chasing, she lost another 20. Now, at 125 pounds, Carolyn was doing far less cardio but loving her newly shaped shoulders and how strong she felt in everyday activities.

"I wish I'd known about this years ago," she told me. "I was working so hard, but in completely the wrong direction."

Even high achievers like Carolyn can get trapped in movement myths that undermine their success. Here are four of the most common exercise myths that derail many well-intentioned exercise plans:

Myth 1: "Exercise to Lose Weight"

Problem: Exercise is a really *inefficient* way to lose weight. That shocks most people at first, until they think about it. A 30-minute workout burns 200-300 calories, while a restaurant meal can contain 1,200+ calories. This creates a transactional mindset: "I earned this dessert because I worked out." When weight loss doesn't happen despite exercise efforts, people conclude exercise doesn't work and quit entirely.

Solution: Exercise for metabolic health. Let nutrition handle weight management. When you separate weight loss from metabolic health, both become more achievable. Here are some legit ways you can use movement to your advantage:

- **Post-Meal Movement:** Movement after eating can cut your blood sugar spike in half.[9] This simple practice stabilizes energy, reduces cravings, and decreases insulin demand throughout the day. Even a gentle 10-15 minute walk produces this benefit. The key is timing the movement shortly after finishing your meal, not hours later.

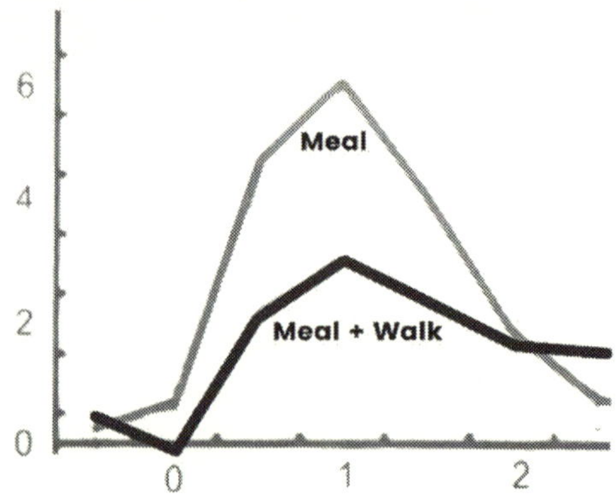

Walking after a meal can cut blood sugar spikes in half compared to sitting still.[9]

Adapted from Manohar C, Levine JA, Nandy DK, et al. The Effect of Walking on Postprandial Glycemic Excursion in Patients with Type 1 Diabetes and Healthy People. Diabetes Care. 2012;35(12):2493-2499. doi:10.2337/dc11-2381

- **Workday Movement:** Sitting for long stretches shuts down your metabolic systems. Brief movement breaks, even just standing and stretching for a minute, keep your body's glucose uptake active and prevent the slowdown that comes with prolonged stillness. Simple activities like taking stairs, walking to a colleague's office, or doing desk stretches maintain your body's engagement throughout the day.

- **Strength Training:** Building muscle creates a metabolic engine that burns calories even while you sleep. After 30, you naturally lose 3-14% of muscle mass per decade. Strength training reverses this decline while improving insulin sensitivity and blood sugar control. Think of it as an investment in your metabolic future rather than a payment for yesterday's food.

Myth 2: "All-or-Nothing"

Problem: The "go hard or go home" mentality creates burnout, injury, and ignores that even 5-10 minutes of movement provides real benefits. Your body responds to any increase in activity, regardless of duration or intensity.

Solution: Think of exercise like a dimmer switch, not an on-off switch. Some days call for gentle movement, others for moderate effort, and occasionally higher intensity. A 10-minute walk is infinitely better than a skipped 60-minute workout. Here are some times of day to consider adjusting the dimmer switch:

- **Morning Movement:** You can start your day with either gentle or higher-intensity workouts. Both cue your internal clock and set your mind and body up for success the entire day. Even better if you can do it outside in the sunshine.

- **Evening Movement:** After sunset, gentle movement calms rather than stresses your system. Light walking, stretching, or yoga helps lower stress hormones and prepares your body for sleep. If evening is your only window for intense exercise, finish at least 2-3 hours before bedtime to avoid disrupting your sleep.

These first two myths focus on *how much* and *how hard* to exercise. But there are two more myths about *when* and *what types* of movement that are equally important to address. In the next chapter, we'll explore the remaining misconceptions that keep even dedicated exercisers from getting the results they want.

CHAPTER 14

Exercise Myths That Keep You Stuck (Part 2)

Now let's tackle the timing and variety misconceptions that can sabotage even well-intentioned exercise routines.

Myth 3: "One-and-Done"

Problem: Your morning workout doesn't protect you if you sit still for the remaining hours of your waking day. Prolonged sitting creates its own health risks, independent of exercise habits. Movement isn't a vaccine that provides all-day protection with one dose.

Solution: If you're awake, you should be moving. Staying still halts all communication with your body, and systems begin to shut down. It needs a constant flow of energy, not a single transaction. This doesn't mean you have to do formal exercise during work hours. It just means your body needs to engage with brief, regular activity to keep your physiology active and alert.

Myth 4: "But I'm a runner." (or Cyclist, or Lifter...)

Problem: Specializing in one type of movement feels efficient, but it creates dangerous gaps in your health. Dedicated runners might have great cardiovascular endurance, but could be losing muscle. Weightlifters might be strong, but can't get up from the floor easily. Yoga enthusiasts might be flexible, but struggle to run up three flights of stairs without getting winded.

Solution: Build a diversified movement portfolio. Your body needs four distinct types of movement to function well into retirement:

N.E.A.T.: Daily non-exercise movement.

This stands for Non-Exercise Activity Thermogenesis. It's basically all the movement you do outside of formal workouts. Walking around the office, taking stairs, or even fidgeting at your desk. It sounds simple, but this daily movement keeps your metabolism humming and blood sugar stable throughout the day.

Step count is a good way to understand your daily NEAT. Aim for 7,000-10,000 steps per day on average. Don't stress about hitting exactly 10,000. Consistency matters more than perfection. You've heard it before, but it's true: park farther away, take walking calls, and use stairs when possible. These small choices add up to major health returns and help you stay energized for evening family time instead of collapsing on the couch.

Functional Ability: Balance and mobility.

This is your ability to move through daily life with confidence: carrying things, reaching overhead, and maintaining balance on uneven surfaces. After 50, falls become a leading cause of serious injury, but functional movement builds the stability and mobility that keep you steady on your feet.

Three simple tests reveal how you're doing:

The Get-Up Test. Can you sit on the floor and return to standing with ease? Research shows that people who need more supports, such as hands or knees, have higher health risks. Each additional support point increases mortality risk by 21%.

Give it a try. Count how many hands, knees, or other supports you need. A lower score means better function. Need help improving? I made a video tutorial of the get-up, which you can access in the Grow Wellthy Resource Hub.

One-Leg Balance. How long can you stand on one leg? Aim for 60-120 seconds per leg. Your balance predicts fall risk better than most complex assessments, and each additional second of stability reduces your odds of falling by 5%.

Practice it often, like every day, while brushing your teeth or waiting for your coffee to brew. Try it with and without shoes.

Grip Strength. How strong is your grip? This simple measure predicts overall health and life expectancy better than most complex assessments. Strong hands mean you can open jars, carry groceries, and maintain independence in daily tasks.

You can test your grip three ways: hanging test, farmer's carry, and hand gripper. More details in the Move toolkit in the next chapter.

Test yourself often and work on the ones that need improvement so you stay strong, capable, and keep your scores up. Your future self wants to play on the floor with grandchildren, navigate airport terminals with ease, and maintain independence for years to come. Plus, these tests are fun party tricks, too!

Strength Training: Muscle protection and growth.

After 30, you naturally lose 3-14% of muscle mass per decade. Strength training reverses this decline, preserving the metabolic engine that burns calories even while you sleep.

I'm going to give you the same advice I gave my 18-year-old son. If there is one fitness takeaway I hope you learn from me, it's this: "Strength train at least twice a week no matter what and never stop."

Muscle is expensive for your body to maintain, so as soon as you stop using it, your body will toss it. It's a costly mistake that 'future you' will regret. Building muscle takes a lot more time and effort than just maintaining it.

You don't need hours in the gym or massive weights. Consistent resistance training, whether with weights, bands, or bodyweight exercises, maintains bone density, improves insulin sensitivity, and builds the strength for active retirement adventures.

Cardiovascular Fitness: Heart and lung capacity.

Cardio builds your heart and lung capacity, but not all cardio is created equal. Make sure you are tapping into each heart rate zone to stay healthy:

Easy: Walking, gentle cycling. You can hold a conversation. This should be most of your cardio and supports recovery when done daily.

Moderate Effort: Brisk walking, hiking. You're working but can still talk. This builds your aerobic base and should be done several times a week.

High Intensity: Short bursts followed by recovery. It requires more recovery time but builds resilience, so 1-2 times a week is probably enough.

These four types of movement create a complete system. Focusing exclusively on one area while neglecting others is like having a perfectly balanced investment portfolio in stocks but no bonds, real estate, or emergency fund.

You don't need to master all four immediately. Start where you are, focus on what you enjoy, and gradually build across all areas. The goal is to create physical fitness that supports the life you want to live.

Intentional Beats Intensity

Each of the myths above teaches us that movement serves a specific purpose when the right type and timing are used. No more random workouts. Give each bout of movement a job. This approach makes exercise more effective while requiring less effort.

Movement doesn't require perfection or extreme measures. The most successful people (and those with higher Continuum scores) focus on consistency, intentionality, and sustainability rather than getting trapped in these common misconceptions.

CHAPTER 15

Move Toolkit

Remember Mark's transformation? He didn't overhaul his life overnight. He made strategic shifts from random intensity to purposeful movement, matching his activities to his goals and working with his body's natural rhythms.

Mark's breakthrough came when he realized he'd been approaching exercise like day-trading instead of retirement planning. He was chasing short-term results with unsustainable intensity instead of building long-term physical resilience.

You now understand the types of movement that matter, how to avoid the common myths, and which approach builds lasting strength. Let's transform these concepts into a movement practice that serves you for decades.

Your Move Assessment

Rate your MOVE health by scoring yourself on four questions:

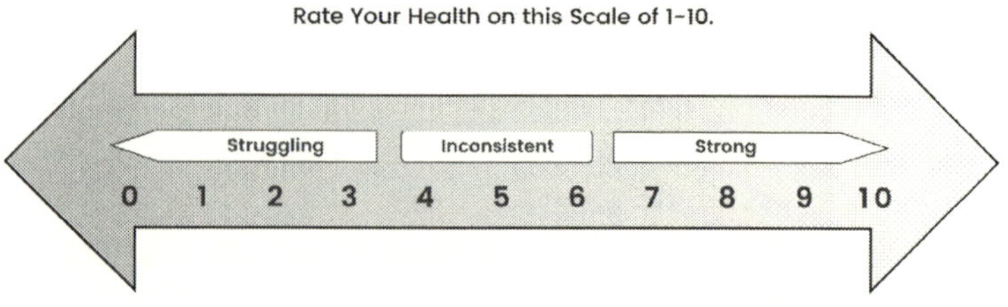

1. _____ How active are you throughout the day?

1-3 = Sedentary lifestyle, under 3,000 steps daily

4-6 = Somewhat active, 3,000-7,000 steps daily

7-9 = Active lifestyle, 7,000-10,000+ steps daily

10 = Highly active, 10,000+ steps effortlessly

2. _____ How well does your body function for daily activities?

1-3 = Significant limitations, poor Get-Up/Balance scores

4-6 = Some limitations, declining function

7-9 = Good function, minor limitations only

10 = Excellent function, perfect Get-Up/Balance scores

3. _____ How consistent is your cardiovascular fitness?

1-3 = No cardio routine, get winded easily

4-6 = Sporadic cardio, inconsistent endurance

7-9 = Regular cardio routine, good heart/lung fitness

10 = Optimized cardio program, excellent endurance

4. _____ How consistent is your strength training?

1-3 = No strength routine, losing muscle mass

4-6 = Sporadic strength work, inconsistent gains

7-9 = Regular strength training, maintaining/building muscle

10 = Optimized strength routine, excellent muscle health

_____ Total / 4 = _______ MOVE Score

Your Movement Action Plan

Test your current ab:

- **Get-Up Test** (count supports needed)
- **One-Leg Balance** (time each leg)
- **Grip strength** (pick the one)
    - Hanging (aim for 30+ seconds for women, 60+ seconds for men).
    - Farmer's Carry (hold dumbbells in each hand for one minute; aim for women 1/3 of body weight in each hand, men about ½ of body weight in each hand).
    - Hand Gripper (aim for 65+ pounds for women, 110+ pounds for men, though it varies with age)

- **Track your baseline activity**
  - Record daily steps for one week (aim for 7,000-10,000 average per day)
  - Note energy levels throughout the day
- **Build your movement portfolio**
  - Schedule strength training at least twice per week
  - Add post-meal walks when possible
  - Set an hourly movement reminder during work

You've Invested in Your Muscle and Function

A consistent, well-rounded movement portfolio builds your best future. It's like the 401(k) of your health. And it completes the four levels of the Hierarchy of Wellth. You have a simple system for building sustainable health that works with your analytical mind and busy schedule.

Each level reinforces the others, creating compound returns on your health investments. With your movement practices in place, you're ready to integrate everything into a personalized system that makes healthy choices feel effortless.

The real magic happens when all four levels work together. In the final section, you'll learn how to weave Mind, Mend, Meals, and Move into daily routines that fit your real life.

Move Takeaways

1. **Exercise for Health, Not Weight Loss:** Let nutrition handle weight management while movement builds strength, independence, and longevity.

2. **Four Movement Types Build Complete Health:** N.E.A.T. (daily movement), functional training (protection), strength training (growth), and cardio (endurance) each serve unique purposes.

3. **Balance Your Movement Portfolio:** Like financial diversification, spreading effort across all four types creates the most resilient health.

4. **Strength Training is Non-Negotiable:** Consistent resistance training reverses age-related muscle loss and boosts metabolism.

5. **Timing Transforms Results:** When you move matters as much as how you move for achieving your health goals.

6. **Post-Meal Walks Cut Blood Sugar in Half:** Simple 10-15 minute walks after eating provide powerful metabolic benefits.

CHAPTER 16

Putting It All Together

You now have all four levels of the Hierarchy of Wellth. You understand how to build awareness and curiosity (Mind), pay your recovery bills (Mend), balance your food budget (Meals), and invest in physical capacity (Move).

But if you're like most high achievers, you might be feeling a familiar sensation: information overload. You know what to do, but you're not sure how to weave it all together into your actual life.

Jennifer thought she had her health planned as carefully as her clients' portfolios.

She approached her health the same way she approached her practice: with research, planning, and determination. She had read the studies, understood the importance of sleep, stress management, balanced nutrition, and regular exercise. She knew she should eat more protein, get better sleep, manage her stress, and exercise regularly.

She bought the books, downloaded the apps, and even hired a trainer. Her Hierarchy of Wellth scores weren't terrible:

- Mind: 6
- Mend: 5
- Meals: 6
- Move: 7

She had some good habits in each area.

Yet after six months of effort, Jennifer felt like she was constantly swimming upstream. Some days she'd nail her morning routine but skip lunch and work until 9 PM. Other days, she'd eat perfectly but skip her workout because a client emergency ran late. She'd have a great week of sleep, then travel would throw everything off for days.

"I know WHAT to do," she told me during our first conversation, exhaustion clear in her voice. "I have all the information. I just can't make it stick. I feel like I'm playing health whack-a-mole. I get one area working, and another falls apart."

Jennifer's frustration is common among high achievers. She had mastered the *what* of health but was missing the crucial *when*. She was doing the right things at the wrong times, fighting against her body's natural rhythms instead of working with them.

What Jennifer discovered changed everything, and it's simpler than you think.

Your Four Daily Windows

Jennifer's breakthrough came when she discovered how important timing is. She moved her workouts from evenings to mornings, started eating her largest meal earlier in the day, and shifted dinner from 8 PM to 6 PM. She began dimming lights after sunset and taking short walks after meals.

Within weeks, everything felt different. The same healthy habits that had felt forced and difficult suddenly felt natural. She was more consistent, her energy rebounded, and she started seeing the results that had been eluding her for months.

"It's like I finally found the rhythm my body was looking for," Jennifer told me. "I'm doing less overall, but everything works better together."

Your body isn't a machine that responds the same way at all hours. It's more like an orchestra, with different systems taking the lead at different times of day. When you eat, move, or rest in harmony with those rhythms, health feels effortless. When you go against them, even the best habits can feel like pushing a boulder uphill.

This is the missing piece that makes everything click.

Instead of remembering dozens of health rules, you can organize your day around four natural windows. Each has its own purpose and optimal practices from the 4M's, and each is backed by your body's daily rhythms.

Organize your healthy habits around four daily windows to tap into the body's natural rhythm.

- **First Hour: Your Wind-Up** Your morning sets the tone for everything that follows. Your body's master clock takes its primary reading here. This is when cortisol naturally peaks to wake you up, insulin sensitivity is highest, and your brain is primed for intention-setting.

- **Work Hours: Your Productivity** This is when your body demands steady energy and focus while still needing movement and stress management. Your metabolic systems slow down with prolonged sitting, but brief interventions keep everything humming.

- **Meal Times: Your Fueling** Your body processes food most efficiently when it expects it. Consistent timing helps regulate hunger hormones, optimize digestion, and stabilize blood sugar throughout the day.

- **Last Hour: Your Wind-Down** Evening routines set up tomorrow's energy, mood, and decision-making. As light dims and temperature drops, your body naturally prepares for the repair and restoration that happens during sleep.

When you align your 4M practices with these windows, something remarkable happens. The benefits start compounding: morning light leads to better sleep at night, better sleep creates sharper afternoon decisions, stable blood sugar provides consistent energy for movement, and movement breaks lower stress and improves focus.

Soon, your days start to reinforce themselves. Each good choice sets up the next.

Understanding these windows is powerful, but here's how to turn this knowledge into your personalized system

Your One-Page Health Plan

Every successful financial advisor knows the power of distilling complex strategies into a single, clear document. You take pages of analysis, market projections, and investment options and create one comprehensive plan that clients can understand and follow.

Here's your health equivalent: The WellthPLAN™, your one-page health plan

This isn't just another wellness chart. This is your central organizing tool. It's the system that makes health feel as systematic and manageable as wealth building. It's the secret sauce that transforms scattered health efforts into an integrated lifestyle.

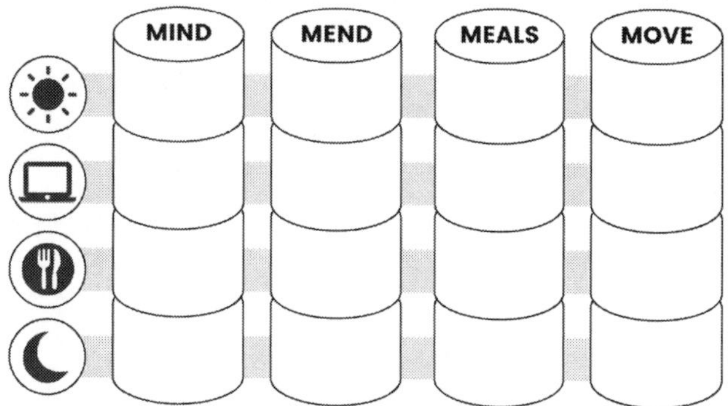

The WellthPLAN™ 4x4 framework offers a simple one-page approach you can customize to your lifestyle.

Looking at your plan, you might think you need to fill out the whole thing and master all 16 touchpoints. You don't.

Remember, you're only as strong as your weakest score. Use the plan to show you exactly where to focus your energy for maximum impact.

Here's how it works: Take your lowest M score from your assessments. Find the daily window that feels most manageable in your current routine. Start there. That intersection becomes your health headquarters and the one practice that anchors everything else.

For example, if your Meals level is your lowest score, pick a simple action for one time of day, such as "first hour," and aim for consistency.

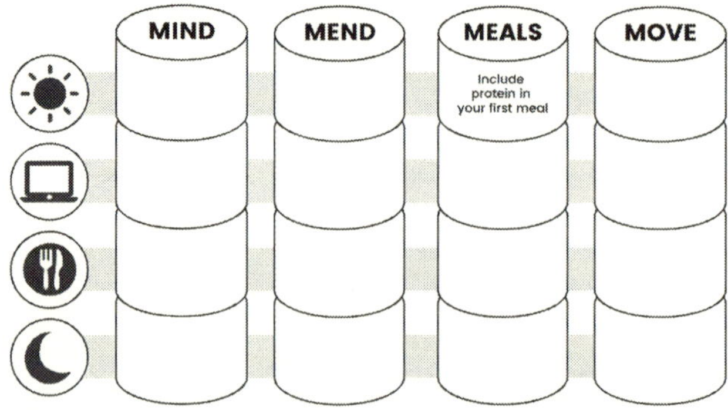

Pick your lowest M score and attach a simple action to a daily window in your WellthPLAN™.

When ready, you can continue building your plan by stacking more Meals habits into other windows of your day. You don't have to do them all every day because you can make significant progress if you do *something* most days.

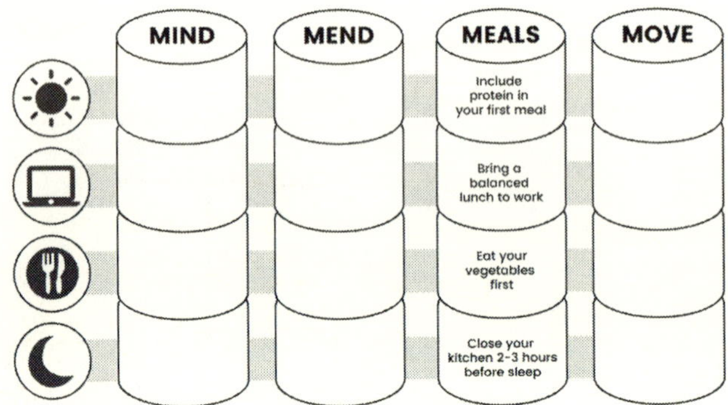

Pick your lowest M score and attach simple actions to each of the four daily windows in your WellthPLAN™.

Once you feel comfortable with that M level, move on to the next M level. If you have multiple levels that are struggling, follow the Hierarchy of Wellth order: Mind, Mend, Meals, Move. Pretty soon, you will have your complete WellthPLAN™ mapped out.

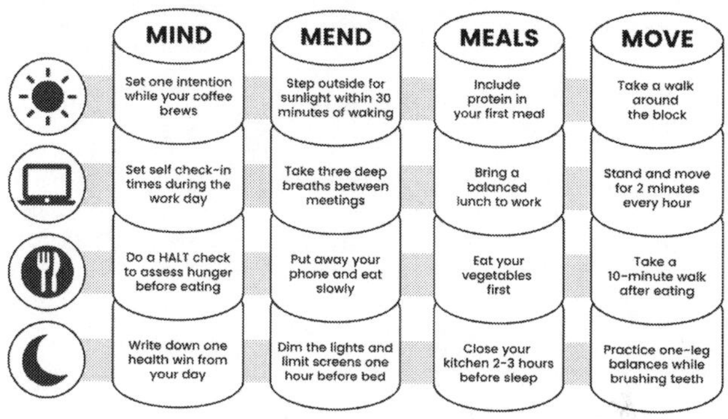

When your WellthPLAN™ is complete, you'll have 16 opportunities to invest in your health each day.

After you've completed your plan, your morning might look something like this:

set intention to stop eating by 8pm → get sunlight → eat protein for breakfast → 15 minute walk

The beauty of this system is its flexibility. Miss your morning routine because of an early flight? Your meal timing and evening practices keep you stable. Dinner runs late because of a client event? Your morning light and movement breaks maintain your momentum.

You're not following a rigid program that breaks the moment life happens. You're living within a framework that bends without breaking.

This is more than a health plan. Your WellthPLAN™ is a life operating system that makes wellness feel as natural and systematic as the financial planning you already do.

When health becomes this integrated, you stop thinking about it as something extra you have to do and start experiencing it as simply how you live.

Your Complete System

Years ago, after my sepsis crisis in Australia, I thought health had to be complicated to be effective. I believed that if I wasn't suffering through intense workouts or restrictive diets, I wasn't trying hard enough.

My body was screaming for help in ways I refused to acknowledge. The sepsis was my body's final, desperate attempt to get my attention.

My lowest score, Mend, wasn't just holding me back; it was literally killing me.

Sleep and stress management weren't luxuries. They were the broken link in my health.

Within three months of focusing primarily on my Mend level, things began to shift. My Mend score climbed from 3 to 7, and my other scores improved, too:

Better sleep → better decision-making → less stress eating → fewer injuries

My overall health score went from 5 to 8. More importantly, I felt like myself again: energetic, clear-thinking, and resilient. My pre-diabetes reversed, and I lost the 20 pounds I had gained.

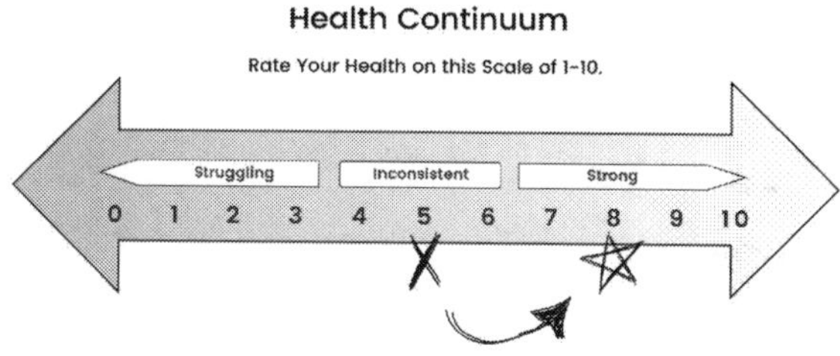

My health improved when I focused on my lowest level - Mend.

The framework that helped me rebuild my health is the same one you now hold in your hands. It works because it focuses your energy where it will have the biggest impact: your weakest link.

Each of the four levels of the Hierarchy of Wellth is critical to your long-term health. Remember that sequence matters more than intensity, and timing matters more than perfection.

The WellthPLAN™ gave me something I'd never had before: a way to be healthy that worked *with* my life instead of against it. I had a way to build lasting health and a framework to organize it all.

The WellthPLAN™ will give you the confidence that comes from approaching health the same way you approach wealth: systematically, strategically, and sustainably.

This is how you grow wellthy. This is how you protect your most valuable asset while building the life you want.

In the next chapter, we'll look at how to protect it when life gets messy.

CHAPTER 17

Navigating Real Life

I had some international travel with a big presentation coming up recently. The pressure was intense because it was a career-defining moment. I found myself working until 10 PM three nights in a row, grabbing dinner at my desk, skipping my evening routine entirely. By day three, I was exhausted, stressed, and feeling like I was failing at my own system.

The old me would have thrown in the towel completely. "I'm a fraud," I would have thought. "I can't even follow my own advice." But not anymore. After years of doing this, instead of abandoning everything, I reminded myself that this is exactly what the system is designed for. Not perfection, but resilience.

You've built your WellthPLAN™. You've taken your first steps. You're making progress. But then life happens, just like it did for me.

A client's emergency keeps you at the office until 9 PM. Your flight gets delayed. Your child gets sick. A market downturn has you working weekends.

You *will* face setbacks. The most consistent thing about life is inconsistency. The question isn't whether obstacles will arise, but whether you'll adapt or abandon your system when they do.

The Most Common Roadblocks

"I Travel a Lot"

The Challenge: Hotel rooms, airport food, disrupted schedules, and client dinners make routines feel impossible.

The Solution: Create travel versions of your core routines.

First Hour: Drink water from the hotel bottle, step outside for 2 minutes, set an intention for your day.

Work Hours: Stand during phone calls, take stairs in hotels, do desk stretches between meetings

Meal Times: Order vegetables first at restaurants, eat slowly during business dinners, walk after meals when possible

Last Hour: Dim hotel room lights, write down one win, prepare for tomorrow

The principles remain the same. The actions adapt to your environment.

"Market Volatility Disrupts Everything"

The Challenge: When markets are crazy, you work longer hours, stress spikes, and healthy habits feel like luxuries you can't afford.

The Solution: Develop emergency protocols, simplified versions of your routines.

During high-stress periods:

- Don't skip meals
- Move more, not less
- Protect sleep above all else
- Use breathing techniques between client calls

These aren't times to abandon health habits. This is when you need them most.

"My Family Environment Isn't Supportive"

The Challenge: Your spouse rolls their eyes at your morning routine. Your kids complain about healthier meals. Family gatherings revolve around unhealthy traditions.

The Solution: Include rather than exclude.

- Invite family members on evening walks
- Involve kids in meal prep
- Model healthy choices without preaching

- Have honest conversations about why this matters to you

A healthier you benefits everyone around you. You're not being selfish—you're being responsible.

"I Don't Control My Schedule"

The Challenge: Back-to-back meetings, unexpected emergencies, and demanding clients leave no room for health habits.

The Solution: Focus on the margins you do control.

You likely have influence over:

- How you start your morning (even 5 minutes counts)
- What you eat and drink during the day
- Your movement between meetings
- How you wind down in the evening

Even small actions in these windows create momentum and prevent complete derailment.

Your Roadblock Recovery Protocol

When obstacles arise, use this three-step process:

Step 1: Assess the Situation

Ask yourself:

- Is this temporary or permanent?

- What parts of my routine can I still do?

Step 2: Adapt, Don't Abandon

Choose one element from each level to maintain:

- Mind: Daily intention-setting (takes 30 seconds)
- Mend: Deep breathing when stressed (works anywhere)
- Meals: Eating vegetables first (possible in any setting)
- Move: Standing every hour (minimal time requirement)

Step 3: Plan Your Return

Roadblocks are temporary. Plan how you'll gradually rebuild:

- Which habit will you restart first?
- What environmental changes need to happen?
- How will you anchor your returning habits?

Your WellthPLAN™ is Built for This

Your system is designed for this reality. It gives you multiple pathways to maintain health even when some routes are blocked. When travel disrupts your morning routine, your meal timing and movement habits keep you stable. When stress affects your sleep, your breathing practices and nutrition support your recovery.

Resilient people don't have fewer problems. They have better get-back-in-the-saddle strategies.

Your Long-Term Success Strategy

Consistency over perfection. Adaptation over abandonment. Progress over paralysis.

Your health journey isn't a straight line. Some days you'll execute 80% of your plan. Other days, you might manage 20%. Both are wins if you keep showing up and adapting.

Those who succeed long-term aren't the ones with perfect circumstances. They're the ones who've learned to thrive in the midst of imperfection.

That's anti-fragile health. That's your path forward.

Conclusion: Your Wellthy Future

"I don't even think about it anymore. I just do it."

This advisor heard me speak at a conference and messaged me six months later about his 30-pound transformation. But it didn't stop there. After asking how he could bring this conversation to his clients, his firm now offers health-wealth content through my Wellth Webinar™ series.

Now his clients tell him, "No other advisor has ever given me this information before. I lost 10 pounds after doing some of the things from that webinar you sent me."

This is what happens when advisors take charge of their health. They become living proof that transformation is possible. Their energy changes. Their presence deepens. Their value expands beyond portfolio management to life optimization.

Your Legacy of Wellth

The work you do with your own health creates ripples far beyond personal transformation. I saw this with Leslie and Tom, whose WellthPLAN™ journey sparked unexpected conversations at their dinner table.

Their teens started asking questions about the family's eating habits, stress management, and sleep routines. Leslie realized they had unconsciously inherited patterns from previous generations: celebrating with sweets, managing stress with alcohol, normalizing sleep deprivation, and treating exhaustion as a badge of honor.

Now their kids watch them choose morning walks over phone scrolling. They're learning that stress doesn't require food or alcohol to manage. They're seeing that energy comes from recovery, not caffeine.

Leslie and Tom's health transformation became their family's generational inheritance. They broke cycles that had persisted for decades and created new patterns their children will carry forward.

The Movement is Growing

Something remarkable is happening in the financial advisory world. The health-wealth connection has moved beyond an idea. It's becoming a movement.

Mark Hedderman, CFP®, Board Member of Financial Planners of Ireland (FPI), heard me on Michael Kitces' podcast and started making changes in his own life. Then his organization did something extraordinary. They invited me to speak at their national conference and moved the entire event from the city to a country wellness retreat.

That decision sent a powerful message: health matters as much as wealth in this profession.

Now I'm meeting clients in person for the first time at conferences across the globe: in Ireland, Barcelona, and beyond. Advisors who started their own health transformations are now championing this message within their firms, mentoring their peers, and integrating wellbeing into wealth planning conversations.

The tide is turning. Industry leaders are paying attention. Advisors are speaking up at conferences, firms are building health into their cultures, and the conversation is spreading from advisor to advisor, firm to firm, country to country.

Your commitment to health influences:

- **Your family** - who sees daily examples of prioritizing wellbeing
- **Your clients** - who feel the difference in your energy and presence
- **Your team** - who benefits from your improved decision-making and resilience
- **Your community** - where you become a catalyst for positive change

When you treat your health like an asset, you give others permission to do the same. And when leaders like Mark step forward, they create space for entire industries to transform.

Who's next? Perhaps it's you.

A Personal Note

This journey is deeply personal for me. What began as a crisis in that Australian hospital became the catalyst for discovering my life's work.

I thought I was healthy until I wasn't. My near-death experience forced me to reimagine everything I knew about wellness. The framework that emerged from my recovery became the roadmap for helping others avoid the same trap.

Everything in my life prepared me for this work: growing up as a financial advisor's daughter, my education in exercise physiology, my health crisis and recovery. All so I could serve advisors who are exactly where I was, successful on paper but struggling with the fundamentals of wellbeing.

What a privilege it has been to work with this community. You are generous, driven, and committed to helping others build better lives. Now I invite you to apply that same dedication to *yourself.*

Health challenges will come as you age. That's simply part of life. What matters is how you meet them. Will you face them with strength, energy, and resilience?

You have the knowledge. You have the framework. You have everything you need to build sustainable wellbeing that enhances every aspect of your life and work.

The choice is yours. And it starts with how you treat your health today. Your most valuable asset is waiting for your investment.

~ the girl named Stevyn

Your Wellthy Future Starts Now

Are you ready to personalize everything you've learned? While this book gives you the frameworks, there are other resources that can support your journey to health.

Grow Wellthy Resource Hub

I've created a companion resource hub to help you implement the concepts in this book. **CoachStevyn.AI** is your personal health planning assistant who can walk you through the steps in a way that works for your unique situation. Think of it as having a health coach available 24/7 to answer your specific questions and guide your implementation. Visit the Resource Hub at
www.growwellthybook.com/resources or scan the QR code below:

1-1 Wellness Consultation

If you'd like more personalized guidance, you can book a Wellness Consultation with me. We'll assess your current health, identify your highest-leverage changes, and see if working together makes sense.
Book a complimentary consultation at
www.growwellthy.com/calendar or scan the QR code below:

References

1.Murphy S, Kochanek K, Xu J, Arias E. *Mortality in the United States, 2023 Key Findings Data from the National Vital Statistics System.*; 2024. https://www.cdc.gov/nchs/data/databriefs/db521.pdf

2.Edward Jones, Age Wave. *Longevity and the New Journey of Retirement.*; 2022. Accessed April 6, 2025. https://www.edwardjones.com/sites/default/files/acquiadam/2022-05/AgeWaveReportMay2022.pdf

3.Greenwald & Associates, Employee Benefit Research Institute. *2019 Retirement Confidence Survey Summary Report.*; 2019. https://www.ebri.org/docs/default-source/rcs/2019-rcs/2019-rcs-short-report.pdf

4.Merrill Lynch, Age Wave. *Health and Retirement: Planning for the Great Unknown a Merrill Lynch Retirement Study Conducted in Partnership with Age Wave.*; 2014. https://agewave.com/wp-content/uploads/2016/07/2014-ML-AW-Health-and-Retirement_Planning-for-the-Great-Unknown.pdf

5.Jones R. Financial Services Rated Most Stressful Industry to Work in. Financial Reporter. Published March 21, 2018. https://www.financialreporter.co.uk/finance-news/financial-services-rated-most-stressful-industry-to-work-in.html

6.Webber A. Financial Services Staff "more Stressed than in 2008 Financial crisis." Personnel Today. Published April 6, 2020. Accessed April 6, 2025. https://www.personneltoday.com/hr/financial-services-staff-more-stressed-than-in-financial-crisis/

7.Attia P, Gifford B. *Outlive.* Harmony; 2023.

8.Means C, Means C. *Good Energy.* Penguin; 2024.

9.Manohar C, Levine JA, Nandy DK, et al. The Effect of Walking on Postprandial Glycemic Excursion in Patients with Type 1 Diabetes and Healthy People. *Diabetes Care.* 2012;35(12):2493-2499. doi:https://doi.org/10.2337/dc11-2381

10.Diaz KM, Howard VJ, Hutto B, et al. Patterns of Sedentary Behavior and Mortality in U.S. Middle-Aged and Older Adults. *Annals of Internal Medicine.* 2017;167(7):465. doi:https://doi.org/10.7326/m17-0212

11.Levine JA. Non-exercise Activity Thermogenesis. *Proceedings of the Nutrition Society.* 2003;62(3):667-679. doi:https://doi.org/10.1079/pns2003281

12.Guo T, Zhou Y, Yang G, et al. Associations of Daily Step Count with all-cause Mortality and Cardiovascular Mortality in Hypertensive US adults: a Cohort Study from NHANES 2005-2006. *BMC Public Health.* 2025;25(1):129. doi:https://doi.org/10.1186/s12889-024-21216-y

13.Paluch AE, Gabriel KP, Fulton JE, et al. Steps per Day and All-Cause Mortality in Middle-aged Adults in the Coronary Artery Risk Development in Young Adults Study. *JAMA Network Open.* 2021;4(9):e2124516. doi:https://doi.org/10.1001/jamanetworkopen.2021.24516

14. de Brito LBB, Ricardo DR, de Araújo DSMS, Ramos PS, Myers J, de Araújo CGS. Ability to Sit and Rise from the Floor as a Predictor of all-cause Mortality. *European Journal of Preventive Cardiology.* 2012;21(7):892-898. doi:https://doi.org/10.1177/2047487312471759

15. Cristina D, Caroline A, Magnani PE, et al. Standing Balance Test for Fall Prediction in Older adults: a 6-month Longitudinal Study. *BMC Geriatrics.* 2024;24(1). doi:https://doi.org/10.1186/s12877-024-05380-9

16. Rezaei A, Bhat SG, Cheng CH, Pignolo RJ, Lu L, Kaufman KR. Age-related Changes in gait, balance, and Strength parameters: a cross-sectional Study. *PLoS ONE.* 2024;19(10):e0310764-e0310764. doi:https://doi.org/10.1371/journal.pone.0310764

17. Fu L. More than 72% of Rookie Advisors Still Fail out of the Industry: Cerulli. AdvisorHub. Published June 27, 2023. Accessed May 27, 2025. https://www.advisorhub.com/more-than-72-of-rookie-advisors-still-fail-out-of-the-industry-cerulli/

18. 2019-The_War_on_Stress. Onefpa.org. Published 2019. Accessed May 27, 2025. https://www.onefpa.org/business-success/ResearchandPracticeInstitute/Pages/2019-The_War_on_Stress.aspx

19. Moody K. Most Finance Pros Say They Plan to Leave the Industry over burnout, Culture. HR Dive. Published July 18, 2024. https://www.hrdive.com/news/finance-pros-plan-to-leave-industry/721720/

20. Fan M, Yuan J, Zhang S, et al. Association between Outdoor Artificial Light at Night and Metabolic Diseases in middle-aged to Older Adults—the CHARLS Survey. *Frontiers in Public Health.* 2025;13. doi:https://doi.org/10.3389/fpubh.2025.1515597

21. Franck M, Tanner KT, Tennyson RL, et al. Nonuniversality of Inflammaging across Human Populations. *Nature Aging*. Published online June 30, 2025. doi:https://doi.org/10.1038/s43587-025-00888-0

22. Younossi ZM, Henry L. Understanding the Burden of Nonalcoholic Fatty Liver Disease: Time for Action. *Diabetes spectrum*. 2024;37(1):9-19. doi:https://doi.org/10.2337/dsi23-0010

23. CDC. Mortality in the United States, 2022. www.cdc.gov. Published March 21, 2024. https://www.cdc.gov/nchs/products/databriefs/db492.htm

24. World Health Organization. World health statistics 2023: monitoring health for the SDGs, sustainable development goals. WORLD HEALTH ORGANIZATION. Published May 19, 2023. https://www.who.int/publications/i/item/9789240074323

25. Office of Disease Prevention and Health Promotion. Healthy People 2030. Healthy People 2030. Published 2024. https://odphp.health.gov/healthypeople

26. Garmany A, Terzic A. Global Healthspan-Lifespan Gaps among 183 World Health Organization Member States. *JAMA Network Open*. 2024;7(12):e2450241-e2450241. doi:https://doi.org/10.1001/jamanetworkopen.2024.50241

27. Watson KB, Wiltz JL, Nhim K, Kaufmann RB, Thomas CW, Greenlund KJ. Trends in Multiple Chronic Conditions Among US Adults, By Life Stage, Behavioral Risk Factor Surveillance System, 2013–2023. *Preventing Chronic Disease*. 2025;22. doi:https://doi.org/10.5888/pcd22.240539

28. World Health Organization. No Level of Alcohol Consumption Is Safe for Our Health. World Health Organization. Published January 4, 2023. https://www.who.int/europe/news/item/04-01-2023-no-level-of-alcohol-consumption-is-safe-for-our-health

29. National Cancer Institute. Alcohol and Cancer Risk. National Cancer Institute. Published July 14, 2021. https://www.cancer.gov/about-cancer/causes-prevention/risk/alcohol/alcohol-fact-sheet

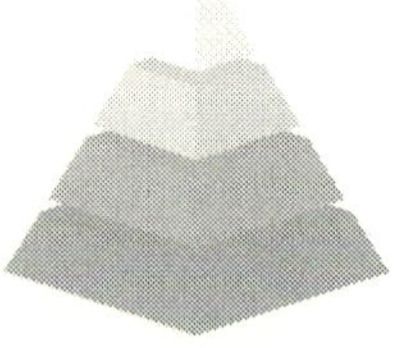

About The Author

Stevyn Guinnip, MS, CWC, is an author, health coach, and international speaker dedicated to helping financial advisors and their clients live well longer. After surviving a personal health crisis, she founded Grow Wellthy™ to merge her expertise in exercise physiology with her firsthand understanding of the financial world as a financial advisor's daughter. Today, she speaks globally, coaches advisors, and equips firms with strategies to protect health as the true retirement multiplier. Stevyn lives in Portugal with her husband and two children.

Made in United States
Orlando, FL
29 November 2025

73409992R00104